KOREAN WAR
CHINESE INVASION
PEOPLE'S LIBERATION ARMY CROSSES THE YALU
OCTOBER 1950—MARCH 1951

GERRY VAN TONDER

Pen & Sword
MILITARY

AN IMPRINT OF PEN & SWORD BOOKS LTD.
YORKSHIRE – PHILADELPHIA

First published in Great Britain in 2020 by
PEN AND SWORD MILITARY
an imprint of
Pen and Sword Books Ltd
47 Church Street
Barnsley
South Yorkshire S70 2AS

Copyright © Gerry van Tonder, 2020

ISBN 978 1 52677 809 3

The right of Gerry van Tonder to be identified as the author of this work
has been asserted in accordance with the Copyright, Designs and Patents Act 1988.

Typeset by Aura Technology and Software Services, India
Printed and bound in Malta by Gutenberg

Pen & Sword Books Ltd incorporates the imprints of Pen & Sword
Archaeology, Atlas, Aviation, Battleground, Discovery, Family History, History, Maritime, Military,
Naval, Politics, Railways, Select, Social History, Transport, True Crime, Claymore Press, Frontline
Books, Leo Cooper, Praetorian Press, Remember When, Seaforth Publishing and Wharncliffe.

For a complete list of Pen and Sword titles please contact
Pen and Sword Books Limited
47 Church Street, Barnsley, South Yorkshire, S70 2AS, England
email: enquiries@pen-and-sword.co.uk
website: www.pen-and-sword.co.uk

or
Pen and Sword Books
1950 Lawrence Rd, Havertown, PA 19083, USA
email: uspen-and-sword@casematepublishers.com
www.penandswordbooks.com

CONTENTS

GLOSSARY

CCP	Chinese Communist Party
CIA	Central Intelligence Agency (US)
CPVA	Chinese People's Volunteer Army
DPRK	Democratic People's Republic of Korea (North Korea)
EUSAK	Eighth United States Army in Korea
FAB	field artillery battalion
FEAF	Far East Air Forces (US)
GIAP	Guards Interceptor Air Regiment (Soviet)
HE	high explosive
IAD	Interceptor–fighter Air Division (Soviet)
IAK	Fighter Air Corps (Soviet)
IAP	Interceptor–fighter Air Regiment
JOC	Joint Operations Centre
JCS	Joint Chiefs of Staff (US)
KATUSA	Korean Augmentation to the US Army
KMAG	Korea Military Advisory Group (US)
KPA	Korean People's Army (North Korean)
MLR	main line of resistance
MSR	main supply route
PLA	People's Liberation Army (China)
PLAAF	People's Liberation Army Air Force (China)
PRC	People's Republic of China
RCT	Regimental Combat Team
ROK	Republic of Korea (South Korea)
ROKA	Republic of Korea Army (South Korean)
TF	task force
UNC	United Nations Command
USMC	United States Marine Corps

It will be noticed that many Korean names of places and geographical features either carry the same suffix or end in the same few letters. These define what a name is being applied to, e.g. Ch'ŏng*ch'ŏn* would be Ch'ŏng River: *ch'ŏn* or *gang* river; *do* island; *dong* town or village within a district or *ri*; *ni* town; *ri* town and surrounding district; *san* mountain.

TIMELINE

1910
Korea is annexed to the Japanese Empire.

1945
15 August: Japan surrenders. US President Harry S. Truman issues a General Order partitioning Korea at the 38th Parallel to facilitate Soviet and American occupying forces to disarm and demobilize the Japanese.
24 August: Soviet troops complete the occupation of their northern half of Korea.
8 September: US occupation forces arrive in Korea.

1947
14 November: The United Nations establishes the UN Temporary Commission on Korea (UNTCOK) for the sole purpose of supervising a general election throughout Korea.

1948
12 January: UNTCOK establishes its headquarters in the Seoul.
23 January: Soviet occupation forces block United Nations Commission on Korea (UNCOK) from entering North Korea.
10 May: UNTCOK supervises a general election held in South Korea.
15 August: An elected government of the Republic of Korea is formed.
12 December: The UN General Assembly recognizes the government of the Republic of Korea as the only lawful government in Korea. The permanent UN Commission on Korea is activated.
26 December: Soviet troops complete their withdrawal from North Korea.

1949
The US, Britain, Canada, New Zealand and Australia recognize the Republic of Korea.
29 June: American occupation forces complete their evacuation of South Korea.

1950
25 June: Massed Soviet-trained and -equipped North Korean forces invade the south.
26 June: The UN Security Council condemns the North Korean attack as a threat to regional peace and international security, calling on P'yŏngyang to withdraw back north of the 38th Parallel.
27 June: The UN Security Council calls upon all its member states to support South Korea. US President Harry S. Truman orders air and naval forces to support the south.

28 June: The South Korean government vacates the capital, Seoul.

29 June: Elements of the Royal Navy and the Royal Australian Navy arrive in Korean waters.

1 July: The UN creates a unified command and General Douglas MacArthur is appointed Commander-in-Chief.

14 July: South Korean forces are placed under the UN command.

20 July: Taejon falls to the North Koreans.

21 July: Canadian transport aircraft arrive in Korea.

30 July: Royal Canadian Navy forces arrive in Korean waters. The Naktong River defence line is established.

1 August: Royal New Zealand ships arrive in Korean waters.

28 August: The British 27th Infantry Brigade under Brigadier Basil A. Coad arrives at Pusan.

15 September: US-led UN forces launch an amphibious landing at Inch'ŏn.

16 September: UN forces commence a breakout from the defensive Pusan Perimeter.

28 September: UN forces liberate Seoul. The Royal Australian Regiment arrives in Korea.

1 October: South Korean forces cross the 38th Parallel into North Korea.

2 October: China threatens to intervene if UN forces enter North Korea.

7 October: The UN authorizes UN forces to pursue the retreating North Korean army into North Korea.

16 October: The Chinese People's Volunteer Army moved invades North Korea from Manchuria.

19 October: P'yŏngyang, capital of North Korea, is taken by UN forces.

26 October: UN forces reach the Yalu River border with China, where Chinese forces are engaged. US forces land at Wŏnsan on the Korean east coast.

27 October: The Chinese launch their first offensive against UN forces.

1 November: Chinese MiG fighter aircraft cross the Yalu River for the first time.

3–18 November: The British 29th (Independent) Brigade under Brigadier Thomas Brodie arrives at Pusan.

7 November: The Canadian 25th Infantry Brigade starts arriving at Pusan.

20 November: The 60th Indian Field Ambulance arrives in Korea.

24 November: General MacArthur orders his troops to march on the Yalu River.

25 November: The Chinese launch their second offensive.

27 November: Chinese troops penetrate the US Eighth Army line, cutting off the US 1st Marine Division at the Changjin (Chosin) Reservoir.

15 December: UN forces withdraw from Hŭngnam and Wŏnsan to consolidate on the 38th Parallel.

23 December

US Eighth Army commander, Lieutenant General Walton Walker is killed in a vehicle collision. He is succeeded by Lieutenant General Matthew B. Ridgway.

31 December: New Zealand field artillery arrives in South Korea.

1951

4 January: UN forces evacuate Seoul.

25 January: UN forces launch Operation Thunderbolt, advancing on the Han River at Seoul.

1 February: The UN condemns China's invasion of North Korea.

21 February: The US Eighth Army launches Operation Killer in a fresh offensive to the north.

7 March: The US Eighth Army launches Operation Ripper to advance across the Han River.

15 March: UN forces retake Seoul.

31 March: UN forces arrive at the 38th Parallel.

INTRODUCTION

'The attack upon Korea makes it plain beyond all doubt that Communism has passed beyond the use of subversion to conquer independent nations and will now use armed invasion and war.'

US President Harry S. Truman[*]

At 4 a.m., local time Korea, on 25 June 1950, while Washington was shut for the weekend, Marshal Ch'oe Yong-gŏn, supreme commander of the Korean People's Army (KPA), ordered a coast-to-coast armoured and infantry invasion of South Korea. In the first in a series of titles on battles of the Korean War, *North Korea Invades the South: Across the 38th Parallel, June 1950*,[†] the author looks at the causes and immediate outcome of the North Koreans' seemingly unstoppable thrust down the peninsula.

Capturing the South Korean capital, Seoul, three days later, the KPA crossed the Han River in force. Clearly caught totally unawares, the understrength US Far East Command in Japan commenced an immediate airlift of combat elements of the US 24th Division into Korea in an attempt to stem the communist flood.

The US 25th and 1st Cavalry divisions followed, but the North Korean avalanche, spearheaded by armour and artillery, could not be stalled, pushing the Americans and Republic of Korea forces into a small enclave on the south-eastern tip of the peninsula, their backs to the Sea of Japan. In his second title on battles of the Korean War, *North Korean Onslaught: UN Stand at the Pusan Perimeter, August–September 1950*,[‡] the author follows Lieutenant General Walton Walker's desperate mobile defence tactics to keep the strategic port of Pusan out of North Korean hands.

Throughout August, and despite repeated penetrating attacks by five KPA divisions, UN forces hold the Naktong Bulge and the Taegu salient.

In Tokyo, UN forces supreme commander, General Douglas MacArthur, was putting the final touches to his high-risk and daring plan of a US X Corps amphibious landing at the North Korean west coast port of Inch'ŏn. The unmitigated 15 September beachhead success represented a dramatic turnaround in the fortunes of war on the peninsula as the UN alliance took the war to the North Koreans for the first time. The author takes a close look at this landmark event in his third title on battles of the Korean War, *Inchon Landing: MacArthur's Korean War Masterstroke, September 1950*.[§]

---

[*] UN Command, Military Intelligence Section, *Korea, A Summary 25 June 1950–25 April 1952*.
[†] Pen and Sword Books, Barnsley, 2018.
[‡] Ibid.
[§] Pen and Sword Books, Barnsley, 2019.

Possibly driven more by the accolades and state-side adulation rather than by tactical advantage, General MacArthur piled enormous pressure on Washington for authorization to pursue the battered remnants of the KPA across the 38th Parallel and into North Korea. South Korean president Syngman Rhee needed no such approval, and on 30 September unleashed his troops north along the North Korean eastern seaboard in a remarkably swift march on the port city of Wŏnsan.

Almost two weeks later, President Truman gave his executive consent and the US 1st Cavalry Division led the US Eighth Army, with British and Australian attachments, into North Korea, striking for the capital P'yŏngyang. This phase of the Korean War is covered by the author in his fourth title in the series on the conflict: *Korean War: Allied Surge, Pyongyang Falls, UN Sweep to the Yalu.*[*]

On 12 October, three days after the publicity exercise between Truman and MacArthur on Wake Island, the US Central Intelligence Agency (CIA) made what may be argued as its most official report to the White House on the subject of foreign intervention in Korea:

> The Chinese Communist ground forces, currently lacking requisite air and naval support, are capable of intervening effectively, but not necessarily decisively, in the Korean conflict. There are no convincing indications of an actual Chinese Communist intention to resort to full-scale intervention in Korea. After reviewing the factors favoring, and those opposing, Chinese Communist intervention, it is concluded that while full-scale Chinese Communist intervention in Korea must be regarded as a continuing possibility, a consideration of all known factors leads to the conclusion that barring a Soviet decision for global war, such action is not probable in 1950. During this period, intervention will probably be confined to continued covert assistance to the North Koreans.[†]

When Chinese or Soviet forces did not intervene at Inch'ŏn, at the crossing of the 38th Parallel or when UN forces reached the Yalu, the CIA appeared to adopt the assumption that they would not do so at all. The repeated failure to recognize such a possibility would to some extent explain the CIA's insistent assumption in the estimates that the Chinese could not take a decisive part in the war without inevitably pushing themselves and the Soviet Union into a world war.

With Mao Zedong's communist victory over Chiang Kai-shek's Kuomintang forces at the close of 1949,[‡] the Communist Chinese had around two million men under arms, with another two million reservists. Whilst many of these troops were concentrated along the Korean border, during 1950 Mao's armies had also reached the area opposite Taiwan

---

[*] Ibid.

[†] CIA Historical Staff, *Study of CIA Reporting on Chinese Communist Intervention in the Korean War, September–December 1950* (October 1955).

[‡] Gerry van Tonder, *Red China: Mao Crushes Chiang's Kuomintang, 1949* (Pen and Sword Books, Barnsley, 2018

and moved south to the borders of Hong Kong, Indochina and Burma. It was, therefore, perceived by the CIA that all these areas were faced with a new threat.

However, the outbreak of the Korean War was interpreted by the CIA as strictly a move by Moscow in terms of world strategy. The known fact that the P'yŏngyang regime existed only by virtue of Soviet support, and was totally subservient to Soviet influence, gave full credibility to the CIA estimates at the time.

Washington's greatest concern, underpinned by Communist Chinese propaganda out of Beijing and proximate dispositions of the People's Liberation Army (PLA), remained as threats to Nationalist Chinese Taiwan and Japan.

The CIA director's memorandum to President Truman of 1 November now conceded that up to 20,000 Chinese troops had in fact been operating south of the Yalu River, 'organized in task force units ... while the parent units remain in Manchuria'.*

Even then, the memo contended, and in agreement with Chinese propaganda, that the presence in North Korea was to protect the Suiho Hydroelectric Zone on the Yalu from hostile actions, referring to it as a 'limited cordon sanitaire'.

Nearly a week after actual intervention, the CIA, albeit still with some reservation, concurred that the Chinese People's Volunteer Army (CPVA) had the capability of halting further UN advances northward 'through piecemeal commitment of troops' or force 'UN withdrawal to defensive positions farther south by a powerful assault'.†

From early November, US Far East Air Force (FEAF) B-29 and B-26 bombers commenced a fortnight of saturation bombing of the North Korean border buffer zone with Manchuria, to 'destroy every means of communication and every installation, factory, city, and village'.‡

General MacArthur's scorched-earth campaign, which included the use of incendiaries for the first time in the conflict, caused near total destruction of many towns and supply centres in the designated target area. In related operations, bridges over the Yalu River were also bombed.

Aerial reconnaissance was restricted to the limited resources of the 543rd Tactical Support Group, but neither the air force nor the US Eighth Army had sufficient skilled photographic interpreters to examine and draw conclusions from the piles of images taken in the proximity of Yalu River crossings. With only a few aircraft, the US 8th Squadron confined their aerial observations to the roads leading from the Yalu to the US Eighth Army and US X Corps.

Finally, on 21 November, the US Fifth Air Force was ordered to conduct close aerial reconnaissance of the area between the two UN forces. But by this time, preparations to strike north were in an advanced stage.

---

* CIA Historical Staff, *Study of CIA Reporting on Chinese Communist Intervention in the Korean War, September–December 1950* (October 1955).

† Ibid.

‡ Robert Frank Futrell, *The United States Air Force in Korea, 1950–1953* (Progressive Management, 1983).

Above left: Harry S. Truman. (Photo NARA)

Above right: Mao Zedong

Below left: Kim Il-sung. (Photo Karow)

Below right: Joseph Stalin.

On 24 November, two days before the launch of the CPVA's first offensive, the CIA estimated that combined Chinese and North Korean forces were incapable of driving the UN off the peninsula, but had the strength to force the international alliance to defensive positions for 'prolonged and inconclusive operations, such, the Communists might calculate, would lead to eventual withdrawal from Korea'.[*]

Washington's miscalculations of China's intentions became rudely and painfully evident on 26 November when General Lin Biao's 'volunteers', in North Korea since mid-October, fell on the US I and IX corps, while simultaneously jumping off from Tŏkch'ŏn to plough through the Republic of Korea Army (ROKA) II Corps. The following two months witnessed the longest retreat in the history of the American military.

At the end of November, US President Truman publicly announced that the use of the atomic bomb was under consideration to check the Red tide. At the same time, the US Strategic Air Command was placed on alert for an immediate deployment of medium bombers to the Far East. Should they go, it would be with atomic capabilities, or what the Pentagon liked to refer to as 'weapons of mass destruction'.

Through to March 1951, the CPVA launched successive offensives, all the while augmenting the troops in Korea with six armies drawn from the First and Second PLA field armies. The US Eighth Army was forced to withdraw south of the Ch'ŏngch'ŏn River as the US 2nd and 25th infantry divisions faced envelopment and annihilation by eighteen CPVA divisions.

At the Changjin Reservoir, known as Chosin Reservoir on Japanese maps, the US 1st Marine and US 3rd and 7th infantry divisions, and 41 Royal Marine Commando, desperately fought for survival against the CPVA IX and XIII corps.

In quick succession, the UN forces evacuated the North Korea capital P'yŏngyang and the east coast port of Hŭngnam. On 16 December, President Truman declared a national state of emergency. Two weeks later, the communists regained Seoul and the UN Command abandoned Inch'ŏn.

General MacArthur's forces fell back on the 38th Parallel. In three months, the euphoric successes of the bold Inch'ŏn amphibious landing, the breakout from the Pusan Perimeter and the lightning speed with which his troops had reached the Manchurian border at the Yalu River, suddenly meant for nothing. Overwhelmingly superior numbers of Chinese troops, driven by a seemingly crazed Mao-indoctrinated fervour, threatened to clear the whole Korean Peninsula of all UN troops and forcibly unite north and south.

A year after the People's Republic of China declared its existence, its forces were ploughing through North Korea to drive the United Nations forces off the Yalu River. General Peng Dehuai was entrusted with saving Kim Il-sung's regime as a matter of grand strategy: holding Korea would secure Manchuria. Kim with thousands of Koreans had

---

[*] CIA Historical Staff, *Study of CIA Reporting on Chinese Communist Intervention in the Korean War, September–December 1950* (October 1955).

fought hand in hand with the People's Volunteer Army (PVA) in 1949: now it was China's opportunity to reciprocate.

The CPVA's participation in the Korean War was the first and only conflict when Chinese and American-led forces clashed in conventional warfare. Initially, the CPVA, drawn from the PLA, enjoyed the advantage provided by its seasoned commanders, whose combat experience and discipline were very evident. With the stalemate at the 38th Parallel, the PVA's shortcomings became visible, especially when confronted with American determination and superior air support. The indecisive Korean conflict, halted with an indeterminate ceasefire in Panmunjom, would cost the PVA a million soldiers.

1. CHAIRMAN MAO'S VOLUNTEERS

Yet, still more came, and the more you shoot the Chinese,
The more there seems to be to shoot,
In a never-ending parody of insanely stupid, terribly worthless,
Quite courageous acts of raw courage.
Or was it opium, we asked?

'One Time Out of History's Calendar'
Ashley Cunningham-Boothe
Royal Northumberland Fusiliers[*]

With the capitulation of Japan in August 1945 heralding the final end of the Second World War, the massive, ethnically diverse country of China waded into a complicated future. Communist leader Mao Zedong's brand of a people-centred ideology ensured his hold over vast areas of northern China, while Chiang Kai-shek's nationalist regime appeared bent on self-destruction as a miscellany of failures frustrated even his most loyal allies.

The closing stages of the Second World War in Asia was also a Soviet affair. With Berlin captured by the victorious Red Army, ending the war in Europe, the wily Joseph Stalin redirected his military resources toward the Far East. In the north-eastern Chinese puppet state of Manchukuo—'State of Manchuria'—acquired by Japan in 1931, a vast agro-industrial empire had grown in isolation as the war in the Pacific effectively kept the region out of the war. The KwAndong Army, an army group of the Imperial Japanese Army, governed Manchukuo, its chiefs of staff holding the top military and civil administration positions. Originally formed as a garrison to protect the railroads paid for by Japanese banks, over a period of twenty-five years the KwAndong Army outgrew its humble beginnings, peaking at a strength of more than 1.3 million, and assuming an exaggerated importance. It had grown large, impressive, and impotent.

On 9 August, at the same time as a flight of American B-29 heavy bombers delivered 'Fat Man' to Nagasaki, the Soviet Red Army sealed Manchukuo's fate. Slicing across Outer Mongolia, half of a giant military pincer carved a path to encircle the KwAndong Army. The other pincer, ferried by river boats across the Amur and Usuri rivers, barrelled down on the Japanese with violent force, their path softened by the largest Soviet airborne operation of the war. The remnants of the KwAndong Army surrendered en masse, the spoils of Manchukuo wide open for the Soviets to do with as they pleased.

But while the Soviet investment of Manchuria, its proper westernized name, seemed like a timely effort that hastened the war's end, it did give Moscow a perfect opportunity to

---

[*] Ashley Cunningham-Boothe and Peter Farrar, Eds., *British Forces in the Korean War* (British Korean Veterans Association, Halifax, 1997)

return favours, but not to the Americans, whose merchant fleet had delivered millions of tons in lend-lease aid for the past five years. China's government, the Kuomintang (KMT), being so reliant on American support, allowed 50,000 Marines to deploy in Manchuria to help the Soviets disarm and repatriate the resident Japanese population. But an attempt at delivering US Marines to the old imperial capital of Peiping and Qingdao was refused. The Soviets were just as steadfast in holding on to Port Arthur in the Liaodong Peninsula jutting along the rim of the Yellow Sea. As a further affront, the KMT was blocked from reclaiming Manchurian cities, which flew in the face of the Chiang Kai-shek's Treaty of Friendship with the Soviet Union.

Since 1919, agents of the nascent Soviet Union were laying the groundwork for the twentieth century's most daring geopolitical project: bringing communism to its Asian neighbours. In 1945, Moscow's military, wounded but buoyant, became a willing accomplice to the astute Mao Zedong and his People's Liberation Army (PLA), who had spent the last ten years encircled in a remote corner of Shaanxi, their final redoubt after the historic Long March.

In a matter of months, some 300,000 troops, under the veteran PLA commander Lin Biao, crossed over to Manchuria. Experts at manoeuvre and subterfuge, the newly formed

Typical People's Liberation Army soldiers, Langyashan, 1941.

corps was allowed to equip themselves with captured Japanese weapons, and even received training at Kiamusze, a semi-clandestine staging ground near the Sino-Soviet border.

From 1937 to 1945, the civil war between Chinese communist and nationalist waged unabated, displacing between 20 and 30 million civilians. In the aftermath of the Pacific war, Washington stepped in in an attempt to broker a lasting peace. Mao was flown to the capital Chungking for an indecisive conference with Chiang and the KMT leadership. The following January, Mao would participate in another round of talks, this time with US General George C. Marshall, doing his best to broker a power-sharing agreement between the factions.

However, and unknown to the Americans, the Chinese Communists had spent months preparing for all-out war against the KMT. What in previous years had been a genuine ragtag peasant army that travelled by foot was, in the space of less than a year, flush with rifles and machine guns, tanks and artillery, with a total strength of 1.3 million.

By the winter of 1948, the balance of power in northern China was swinging in favour of the People's Liberation Army. As the PLA Fourth Field Army, commanded by Lin Biao and Luo Ronghuan, entered the North China Plain at the close of the Liaoshen Campaign, Fu Zuoyi and the KMT government in Nanking abandoned Chengde, Baoding, Shanhai Pass and Qinhuangdao, while simultaneously withdrawing the remaining Nationalist troops to Beiping, Tianjin and Zhangjiakou to strengthen the defences of these garrisons. On 14 January 1949, the PLA launched a final attack on Tianjin. After twenty-nine hours of bitter fighting, the KMT LXII and LXXXVI corps and a total of 130,000 men in ten divisions were either killed or captured.

The fall of Tianjin effectively left the KMT garrison in Beiping completely cut off from other nationalist forces. On 31 January, the PLA Fourth Field Army marched into Beiping to claim another people's victory, and in doing so, marked the end of the campaign.

With the final demise of the KMT, in June 1949 the CCP announced the ideological methodology for the ultimate neutralization of all KMT structures and what they stood for. In its stead would be the Maoist roadmap. A year later, in Beijing, the new regime would start to pay considerable attention to the ramifications of the ebb and flow of the fortunes of opposing forces locked in combat south of the Yalu River.

Early in October 1950, the CCP politburo convened to consider the potential consequences of intervening in the Korean conflict. Master diplomat and skilled political tactician, Mao's prime minister, Zhou Enlai, had recently met with Soviet ambassador Terentii Shtykov, who informed Zhou that Moscow endorsed the deployment of nine PLA divisions along the Manchurian border with North Korea. There had been an added promise of Soviet air support in the event of an offensive across the Yalu River.

On 8 October, Mao issued a mobilization and deployment order as the instrument to initiate the politburo's decision to intervene in Korea. The order ratified the appointment of Peng Dehuai as commander of the CPVA, the retitled Northeast Border Army. The CPVA would comprise three armies from XIII Corps, commanded by Deng Hua, and one from XIV Corps. The Border Artillery Command would form part of the force, made up of the 1st, 2nd and 8th artillery divisions.

Although the Chinese Reds were represented by a peasant army, it was also a first-rate army when judged by its own tactical and strategic standards. Military poverty might be blamed for some of its deficiencies in arms and equipment, but its semi-guerrilla tactics were based on a mobility which could not be burdened with heavy weapons and transport. The Chinese coolie in the padded cotton uniform could do one thing better than any other soldier on earth; he could infiltrate around an enemy position in the darkness with unbelievable stealth. Only Americans who have had such an experience can realize what a shock it is to be surprised at midnight with the grenades and submachine gun slugs of gnome-like attackers who seem to rise out of the very earth.

Press correspondents were fond of referring to "the human sea tactics of the Asiatic hordes." Nothing could be further from the truth. In reality the Chinese seldom attacked in units larger than a regiment. Even these efforts were usually reduced to a seemingly endless succession of platoon infiltrations. It was not mass but deception and surprise which made the Chinese Red formidable.[*]

[*] L. Montross et al, *U.S. Marine Operations in Korea, 1950–1953* (US Government Printing Office, Washington, 1962).

Peng Dehuai.

Peng was born in Hunan Province, where he enlisted in the army at the age of 18, before graduating from the Hunan Military Academy in August 1923. Early in 1928, he joined the Chinese Communist Party. After becoming one of Mao's closest lieutenants during the Long March of 1935, Peng was appointed deputy commander-in-chief of the PLA in 1937.

At the time, the strength of a PLA corps was between 30,000 and 35,000 soldiers, a division 9,000 to 10,000, a regiment 2,000 to 2,700, a battalion 500 to 530, a company 100 to 120, a platoon 30 to 35, and a squad 9 to 12.[*]

A division, such as the 118th of the CPVA XL Corps,[†] was composed of three regiments: in this case, the 354th, 355th and 356th. Attached to the division was an artillery regiment, a guard company, a special services company, a signal company, an engineer battalion, a stretcher-bearer company, a medical company and a cavalry platoon. Each regiment was equipped with six 122mm mountain guns, twelve 122mm field guns, each battalion with six heavy machine guns and three 120mm mortars, each company with six light machine guns and three 82mm mortars, and each platoon with eight Soviet rifles and two light machine guns.

Mao's military machine was entirely powered by an insistence of 'man-over-weapons'. With political doctrine at its core, the victory of the people's army of the communist revolution against the nationalists was the optimum exploitation and enhancement of the 'human element'. It was a philosophy, founded on the successes of the civil war, that the morale of the Red soldier relies totally on the military structure and doctrine, political controls and social organization to defeat better-equipped enemies. However, the strengths and weaknesses of such a military system would be severely tested in the first eight months of Mao's expedition across the Yalu River:

> CCF [CPVA] attacking force ranged as a rule from a platoon to a company in size, being continually built up as casualties thinned the ranks. Reports by newspaper correspondents of "hordes" and "human sea" assaults were so unrealistic as to inspire a derisive Marine comment: "How many hordes are there in a Chinese platoon?"
>
> After giving CCF tactics due credit for their merits, some serious weaknesses were also apparent. The primitive logistical system put such restrictions on ammunition supplies, particularly artillery and mortar shells, that a Chinese battalion sometimes had to be pulled back to wait for replenishments if the first night's attack failed. At best the infantry received little help from supporting arms.
>
> POW interrogations revealed that in many instances each soldier was issued 80 rounds of small arms ammunition upon crossing the Yalu. This was his total supply. The artillery and mortars were so limited that they must reserve their fire for the front line while passing up lucrative targets in the rear areas. Some attempts were made to bring reserve stocks up to forward supply dumps about

---

[*]   CIA Information Report, 27 October 1951.

[†]   The author uses the more familiar and structurally correct term 'corps' for the military unit that the Chinese refer to as 'army'.

30 miles behind the front, but not much could be accomplished with animal and human transport.

The consequence was a tactical rigidity which at times was fatal. Apparently CCF commanding officers had little or no option below the battalion level. A battalion once committed to the attack often kept on as long as its ammunition lasted, even if events indicated that it was beating out its brains against the strongest part of the opposing line. The result in many such instances was tactical suicide.

After these defects are taken into full account, however, the Chinese soldier and the Korean terrain made a formidable combination. Ironically, Americans fighting the first war of the new Atomic Age were encountering conditions reminiscent of the border warfare waged by their pioneer forefathers against the Indians.[*]

The advent of the People's Republic of China in 1949 brought with it a national army in transition, displaying an enormous internal variation in training, indoctrination, political strength and loyalty, military efficiency and morale. Being fully cognizant—and wary—of such issues, the communist nation's leaders undertook an assiduous selection of the best units from throughout the entire PLA, drawing from the crack Third and Fourth field armies to respond to the situation in Korea. In mobilizing an initial intervention force of 30 divisions, numbering around 300,000 troops, they considered the political strength and reliability of different units as well as the quality of military weapons, training and experience.

Commanded by civil war veteran and staunch Maoist Lin Biao, the PLA Fourth Field Army (formerly Northeast Field Army), generally regarded as being the best of the PLA's five field armies, consisted of the XXXVIII, XXXIX, XL, XIII, XLII and XIV corps, all selected for being especially strong.

The five armies had been bestowed with the honorary title of 'Iron' troops. They had acquitted themselves well in the civil war against better-equipped Nationalist armies. They had subsequently strengthened themselves by assimilating Nationalist POWs who possessed military skills required in the PLA. Of importance was the fact that these armies contained a relatively low proportion of new recruits.

Another constituent element of the PLA Fourth Field Army forming part of the initial intervention force, was L Corps, the erstwhile Nationalist Sixtieth Army. An exception to the complexion of the five true PLA armies, this unit had defected virtually intact to the communists during the civil war. Retitled the L Corps, hardened communists filled all the key positions.

Whilst the PLA Third Field Army as a whole was not considered as strong as the Fourth, the XXVI Corps—also included in the initial intervention force—was a crack unit. The XX and XXVII corps of the Third Field Army also formed part of the strike force. The LXVI Corps, PLA First Field Army, with a reputation for being politically worthy, completed the CPVA expeditionary force.

---

[*] L. Montross et al, *U.S. Marine Operations in Korea, 1950–1953* (US Government Printing Office, Washington, 1962).

Mao' peasant soldiers, Second World War.

Such were the perceived capabilities of the experienced and indoctrinated human element of the CPVA, that Beijing expected a rapid and comparatively easy victory over MacArthur and his UN forces. The communist leadership launched major offensives in late November and on New Year's Day 1951, fully confident that the superior military doctrine, tactics, political loyalty and morale of their best armies would defeat the better-equipped enemy.

However, the initial force failed to accomplish the ambitious objective assigned to it of driving the UN forces off the Korean Peninsula. Following the collapse of the third CPVA offensive in January 1951, their armies withdrew to stronger defensive positions close to the 38th Parallel to regroup and prepare for renewed operations.

At about this time, Beijing made the decision to send fresh troops into Korea. The entire PLA was scoured once more for units considered suitable for combat south of the Yalu. A sizeable new force, this time drawn largely from the PLA First and Second field armies, was selected and sent into Korea.

The VIII Corps had already been deployed to Tibet in 1950, so the XII, XV and LX corps were selected from the PLA Second Field Army for Korea. From the PLA First Field Army, the LXIII, LXIV, LXV and XIX corps, the latter considered to be the strongest after having fought well in the civil war. The remainder of the First Field Army was not held in such high regard. The second contingent of troops sent to Korea also included the XLVII Corps of the PLA Fourth Field Army, another relatively weak force.

Poised on the north bank of the Yalu River, the Chinese soldier was not a volunteer, but a regular member of the PLA. Typically, he was clad in a mustard yellow, quilted, cotton, winter uniform, and to protect his neck and head, a cap with fur-lined ear flaps. His simple and meagre rations, usually of rice, millet or soybeans, were only meant to last four days. Thereafter, he was expected to forage for his own food.

The inured, often illiterate peasant soldier, undertook forced night marches without complaint. Not entitled to even the most basic prophylactic medical care, the enlisted man was expected to live out his life under arms for his country. There was no provision

Our movement of 'Resist U.S. aggression and aid Korea' is just not to allow their calculations based on wishful thinking be realized and, as the old saying goes, 'hit a fist, so to avoid one hundred fists coming'. As you all know, I do not fight a battle when I am not sure of winning. This time, we have decided to send the Volunteer Army abroad, although some people do not agree and believe there is no certainty for winning. But I and some comrades in the Central have carefully studied it, developed a protracted war strategy, and are sure of victory.

We estimate that the army of the imperialist U.S. has one advantage and three weaknesses. It has more steel, more aircraft and more cannons than us, and it is the only advantage it has. But it has many military bases in the world, have enemies everywhere, have to defend everywhere and lack of manpower, which is its first weakness; it is an ocean apart from other countries, which is its second weakness; and it fights for aggression, sending the army out without a righteous cause and its morale is low, which is the third weakness and is fatal. Although there is an advantage, but it cannot match the three weaknesses.

We shall carry on a protracted war, eliminate its effective force step by step, and make it more casualties every day. If it does not retreat on a day, we hit it for the day; if it does not retreat in a year, we hit it in the year; if it does not retreat for ten years, we hit it for the ten years. In this way, the U.S. military will have more and more casualties, and cannot stand any further and then will have to be willing to carry out a peaceful settlement. As long as it is willing to make a peaceful settlement, we can end the war. We want peace from the very beginning.

Mao Zedong[*]

[*] Min Mao, *Marshal Peng De-huai* (2018).

to resign from the PLA—only death or physical incapacity could relieve the individual of his uniformed obligations to the state.

The rifles carried by the CPVA were once the property of the Imperial Japanese Army, confiscated by the Soviet Union in 1945 and handed over to the Chinese communists. Other weaponry, including rifles, grenades, machine guns and bazookas, were American, captured by Mao's army from the defeated nationalists in 1949.

The combat units were arranged in a manner to accommodate disparate regional dialects: men from Manchuria were unable to understand someone from Shanghai. Staff officers preferred the Mandarin dialect. Below the battalion level, communication, rudimentary by Western standards, was conducted with flares, bugles, horns, whistles and by runner.

The basic infantry unit was characterized by a distinctive three-by-three format, ensuring optimum control by the squad leader who was usually a political appointee and instrument. Assuming command of the US Eighth Army in Korea in April 1951, General James A. Van Fleet, said of this system:

> The Red Chinese Army is divided at the very bottom into units of three men, with each assigned to watch the others and aware that they in turn are watching him. Even when one of them goes to the latrine, the other two follow. No soldier dares fail to obey orders or even complain. The little teams of three, each man warily watching the others, begin the advance.

PLA soldiers assigned to protect an artillery position, *c.* 1951.

Yet—although terribly alone in the fight despite the two men at his side, made even more lonely by the doubt whether the two are there to help him or to spy on him—the Red soldier moves ever forward.[*]

Within the rank and file of the PLA material rewards to motivate the soldier were wholly absent. Instead was a well-structured communist political hierarchy, that permeated every level, encouraged and cajoled by extolling the virtues and honours of fighting to defend China. The message gained extra prominence at pre-combat sessions, where squad members were required to sign a solemn pledge:

> We eight members of the squad hereby solemnly promise to be determined to kill the enemy by helping the leader in this combat and achieve merits to our most glorious honour.
>
> I will fight bravely without being afraid of enemy fire and make our firearms effective to the greatest extent.
>
> I will overcome every difficulty. I will not be afraid of great mountains to cross or of long marches. I will fight bravely as usual even when I have nothing to eat for a full day.
>
> We will be united and help one another, observe one another, so that we may not retreat even a step.
>
> We eight members of our squad without fail will kill and wound more than three enemies for the people of China and Korea and for our leader.
>
> Should we fail to do these, we wish to be punished.[†]

Up to this point in history, Western military analysts generally thought little about the capabilities of the Chinese soldier who, in his own country, sits on the bottom rung of the social hierarchy. There was no national military history, but only sporadic conflict by a succession of emperors, warlords and bandit hordes. The fighting man was more often an illiterate peasant pressganged into military service.

Colonel Evans F. Carlson of the US Marine Corps (USMC) had been given special dispensation by the communists to accompany Mao's forces as a foreign military observer. Travelling more than 2,000 miles with the communist guerrillas in 1937 and 1938, Carlson was left with an indelible impression of 'toughness, mobility and uncomplaining endurance of these Chinese soldiers'.[‡] However, the Western world at the time remained unfamiliar with this new breed of Chinese soldier.

---

[*] James McGovern, *To the Yalu: From the Chinese Invasion of Korea to MacArthur's Dismissal* (William Morrow, New York, 1972).

[†] Ibid.

[‡] Ibid.

2. RED PHANTOM

I had slept, not long, the soldier's fractured sleep,
That parked its arse upon the razor's edge of my taut nerves.
Dawn was not yet in the making in God's black opal eye.
Night coalesced the sky with the uncharitable earth and the
Inhospitable mountains,
Making one great, dreadful black of darkness.

'One Time Out of History's Calendar'
Ashley Cunningham-Boothe
Royal Northumberland Fusiliers[*]

In the first few hours of darkness on 19 October 1950, PLA Marshal Peng Dehuai drove across a bridge straddling the Yalu River onto North Korean soil. Four armies from the CPVA XIII and XIV corps crossed the Yalu immediately afterwards. Met by North Korean senior officer Park Xian-yong, Peng was escorted to Datong, a village near the Sup'ung (Shuifeng) Dam hydroelectric power station where he had lengthy talks with North Korean leader, Kim Il-sung.

In his seminal work, *On Protracted War* in 1938, Mao Zedong had defined what would twelve years later form the basis of his military intervention in Korea, and one which Peng conveyed to a relieved Kim:

> Our strategy should be to employ our main forces in mobile warfare over an extended, shifting, and indefinite front, a strategy depending for success on a high degree of mobility in difficult terrain, and featured by the swift attack and withdrawal, swift concentration and dispersal. It will be a largescale war of movement rather than a positional war depending exclusively on defensive works with deep trenches, high fortresses, and successive defensive positions. We must avoid great decisive battles in the early stages of the war, and must first employ mobile warfare gradually to break the morale, the fighting spirit, and the military efficiency of the living forces of the enemy.

From 30 September to 10 October 1950, the 3rd and Capital divisions of ROKA I Corps had ploughed their way at an amazing pace through the KPA 5th, 12th and 15th divisions, northward along the Korean peninsula's east coast. They took the port city of Wŏnsan

---

[*] Ashley Cunningham-Boothe and Peter Farrar, Eds., *British Forces in the Korean War* (British Korean Veterans Association, Halifax, 1997).

USS *Gunston Hall* (LSD-5) en route to Wŏnsan, October 1950. (Photo US Navy)

before the delayed 1st Marine Division, US X Corps, landed from the sea. At the same time, the 6th, 7th and 8th divisions, ROKA II Corps, made slower progress to the north, hindered by the difficult, broken terrain.

On the South Koreans' left flank and west to the coast, the US Eighth Army, with British, Australian and Philippine attachments, met with stronger and better organized enemy units. Spearheaded by the US 1st Cavalry Division, General Walton Walker's men advanced on the North Korean capital, P'yŏngyang, entrapping six enemy divisions south of the 38th Parallel.

Shortly after P'yŏngyang, on 25 October General Walker told correspondents at his headquarters that 'Everything is going just fine.' However, the situation on the ground was of growing concern. General MacArthur had split the command of his US forces: General Walker's US Eighth Army to the west and the US X Corps under Major General Edward Almond to the east at Wŏnsan. Each commander reported directly to MacArthur, making for a high-risk liaison problem. For many a senior staff officer, however, the huge 75-mile gap between the two commands left Walker's right flank exposed and vulnerable, made worse by the 7,000-feet peaks of the Taebaek Range that would prevent one force from going to the aid of the other.

FRESH BRITISH TROOPS HAVE HARD FEET

With 970 officers and men of the 1st Battalion Royal Northumberland Fusiliers on board, the 14,056-ton troopship, Empire Hallidale, sailed from Southampton for Korea yesterday. Army boots rattled along the decks of the ship as she was getting ready to sail. Boots are often taboo on a troopship, but Lieut.-Colonel K.O. Foster, commanding the battalion, received special permission for his men to keep them on, and they will wear them throughout the voyage.

"The object is to prevent the men's feet becoming soft," Colonel Foster explained. "It is certainly most unusual for a troopship, but I am determined that the men will arrive with hard feet."

Colonel Foster had this to say about the morale of the men, mostly reservists from the North of England. "It very high, considering that no one likes being taken from their home and sent to the far corners of the earth." The men have made it clear that they are going to live up to the regimental motto, "Quo Fata Vocant" (Whither the Fates call). The battalion, "The Shiners," landed in Southampton from Gibraltar only eight months ago. Making the ship's complement of 1,400 were 200 men of the 170 mortar battery R.A. commanded by 34-year-old Major T. V. Fisherhoch, more than 100 men of the R.A.O.C., and some R.A.P.C. personnel.

As handkerchiefs fluttered from the quayside and bandsmen rose to their feet for "Auld Lang Syne," the Empire Hallidale sailed dead on time.

Belfast News-Letter, 12 October 1950

On the same day that General Walker assured the western press that everything was 'fine', a ROKA battalion, while advancing rapidly on the Yalu, now only 50 miles away, was stopped dead in its tracks near Onjŏng. Several leading vehicles detonated landmines, causing the South Korean troops to debus to neutralize what was assumed to be yet another pocket of North Korean resistance. However, they were caught in a well-organized ambush, with concentrated machine-gun and rifle fire pouring down on them from high ground. The South Korean battalion ceased to exist as a structured force. As the survivors fled back the 8 miles to Onjŏng, they captured two enemy prisoners. Both were Chinese.

As the first winter snow began to fall on 25 October, at Unsan, a strategic crossroads 45 miles south of the Yalu, the ROKA 1st Division was attacked by an enemy far more powerful than the retreating KPA. A Chinese infantryman was captured and transported to US II Corps HQ, where he informed corps commander Major General Frank Milburn that there were around 20,000 CPVA troops positioned to the east and north of Unsan. The prisoner confirmed he was a serving member of the CPVA 39th Division.

At 3.30 a.m. the following morning, at Onjŏng, 10 miles north-east of Unsan, troops of the 11th and 12th regiments, ROKA 1st Division harboured there were startled awake by the alien sounds of bugles, rams' horns and high-pitched whistles. From the dark, figures in heavily quilted uniforms emerged, firing sub-machine guns and rifles and lobbing grenades. The South Koreans offered no resistance and, panic-stricken, fled into nearby hills. The night assailants were from the 116th Division, CPVA XXXIX Corps.

At first light, a reconnaissance patrol from the 7th Regiment, ROKA 6th Division, arrived at Ch'osan on the south bank of the Yalu, the first of the UN forces to reach the Manchurian border. Here they discovered a footbridge stretching over the river to the north bank. There were no signs of foreign troops, just a stream of North Korean refugees seeking safety in Manchuria. Leaving behind a small detachment, the South Koreans and their Korean Military Advisory Group (KMAG), led by Major Harry Fleming, set off on the 18 miles back to regimental HQ at Kojang. En route, they encountered a roadblock, where they were enveloped and all but totally annihilated. Sustaining fifteen wounds, Fleming was captured, but would succumb to his wounds while a Chinese captive.

Taking note of these incidents, US Eighth Army Intelligence (G2) in its daily report of 26 October concluded that, while it was apparent Chinese troops had been encountered

Chinese machine-gunner.

trying to defend their international border, there were 'no indications of open intervention on the part of Chinese Communist Forces in Korea'.[*]

The next day, ROKA 1st Division commander, 30-year-old Paek Sŏn-yŏp, arrived at Unsan to examine the bodies of dead enemy soldiers killed in the engagement with his men. Having served with the Japanese Manchurian Army during the Second World War, there was no question in his mind that the dead soldiers were in fact of Chinese ethnicity. Investigating the scene further, Paek strongly believed that he was facing a Chinese division of around 10,000 troops.

General MacArthur vetoed any presence of the fledgling Central Intelligence Agency (CIA) in Tokyo or at General Walker's HQ in P'yŏngyang, dogmatically investing all his faith in his G2 chief, Major General Charles A. Willoughby. '[O]nly after the great and catastrophic failure on the whereabouts and intentions of China's armies would the CIA finally be allowed into the region.'[†]

It remains a subject of debate as to the sourcing and rationale behind General Willoughby's intelligence estimates for his much-admired commander, especially with regard to his Far East Command Daily Intelligence Summary in Tokyo on 28 October:

> From a tactical pint of view, with victorious U.S. Divisions in full deployment, it would appear that the auspicious time for such intervention [Chinese] has long since passed; it is difficult to believe that such a move, if planned, would have been postponed to a time when remnant North Korean forces have been reduced to a low point of effectiveness.[‡]

In the US X Corps sector to the east, elements of the ROKA 3rd Division were attacked by a large force near Chosin (Changjin) Reservoir. Sixteen Chinese soldiers were taken prisoner in the fight, a development that division commander Brigadier General Kim Baik Yil immediately signalled to General Almond. Upon his arrival, Almond was able to glean from the prisoners that they had crossed the Yalu during the night of 16 October, and that there were two Chinese divisions in the Chosin area.

General Walker's right flank was now in real danger of being completely exposed as the South Koreans in that sector became increasingly fearful of the Chinese threat. As a consequence, Walker ordered the US 1st Cavalry Division out of reserve to reinforce ROKA forces at Unsan. On 1 November, the US 8th Cavalry Regiment (US 8th Cavalry) arrived at Unsan, still oblivious of the massive Chinese presence in the area. In his report

---

[*] James McGovern, *To the Yalu: From the Chinese Invasion of Korea to MacArthur's Dismissal* (William Morrow, New York, 1972).

[†] David Halberstam, *The Coldest Winter: America and the Korean War* (Hachette Books, New York, 2018).

[‡] James McGovern, *To the Yalu: From the Chinese Invasion of Korea to MacArthur's Dismissal* (William Morrow, New York, 1972).

CPVA soldiers being searched by their US Marine captors. (Photo US Navy)

to the UN Security Council for the period 16–31 October, General Willoughby concluded that 'there was no evidence that Chinese Communist units, as such, have entered Korea'.*

That night—1 November—at around 7.30 p.m., the sound of whistles and bugles heralded the arrival of the hitherto red phantom that was the CPVA. Numbering 20,000 troops, two CPVA divisions struck at the 3,500-strong US 8th Cavalry with a barrage of mortar and rocket fire. To the south at Anju on the Ch'ŏngch'ŏn River, US I Corps commander, Major General Frank W. Milburn, was in conference with Major General Hobart R. Gay, commanding the US 1st Cavalry Division, the commander of the US 24th Division (US 24th), Major General John H. Church, and the commander of the ROKA 1st Division. General Walker had earlier contacted Milburn to warn him that the defeat of the ROKA II Corps to the east had left his right flank vulnerable.

At the conference, Milburn expressed his deep concern that over-extended lines of supply would not be able to support a prolonged engagement with superior numbers of Chinese forces at Unsan. Accordingly, he ordered the 1st and 2nd battalions,

---

* James McGovern, *To the Yalu: From the Chinese Invasion of Korea to MacArthur's Dismissal* (William Morrow, New York, 1972).

North Korean civilians acting as porters for the Chinese invaders.

US 8th Cavalry (US 1/8th Cavalry and US 2/8th Cavalry) to immediately withdraw to a position 12 miles to the south. The US 24th, now only about 20 miles from the Yalu, was ordered to halt its advance on the Manchurian border. For the first time since crossing the 38th Parallel, MacArthur's UN forces had gone from attack to defence.

However, for the two American cavalry battalions, the orders were too late, finding their line of retreat blocked by two divisions of the CPVA XXXIX Corps. In the heavy fighting that ensued, the Americans were unable to breach the CPVA roadblock. Abandoning tanks, artillery pieces and vehicles, survivors bombshelled into nearby hills to find their own way back to the south.

To the south-east, the US 8th Cavalry's 3rd Battalion (US 3/8th Cavalry), commanded by Major Robert Ormond, had been deployed to protect the regiment's rear, blissfully unaware of the fate of its sister battalions. Positioned at a stream dubbed Camel's Head Bend, the battalion was separated from its command post by a bridge over the Nammyŏn River. The crossing was guarded by K and L companies.

At 3.30 a.m. on the morning of 2 November, large numbers of CPVA troops crossed the bridge and fell on the command post with small-arms fire and grenades. Chinese infantry and cavalry—astride hardy Mongolian ponies—wreaked havoc on the slumbering post.

It was a blustery cold but bright day. The snow had ceased to fall and everyone was in good spirits. About ten miles up the road the convoy slowed down and then came to an abrupt halt. It got colder and colder, the men became restive. All kinds of rumors drifted back down from the head of the column. Then came the real dope. Everyone was to dismount, our vehicles were to be used to take the wounded and dead back to Seoul. Everyone wanted to know, what wounded, what dead? The men of Easy Company secured their gear, tightened their belts, and moved in combat formation along the vehicle-choked road. Soon, in the frozen rice paddies along both sides of the road, they passed bodies stacked like cordwood. It didn't take a genius to figure out that one of the 1st Cavalry's units had pulled another Custer.

Sergeant Robert Dews
E Company, US 21st Infantry Regiment

Battalion operations officer, Captain Filmore McAbee, leapt out of the command post dugout, dashing for the bridge. However, taking a hit through his left shoulder and having his helmet shot from his head, McAbee returned to the roadside dugout, where he and battalion executive officer, Major Veale Moriarty, became embroiled in desperate close-quarter fighting with their assailants for almost half an hour.

At first light, USAF fighter-bombers forced the Chinese to break off their attack and take to cover. McAbee and Moriarty survived the ordeal, but the seriously wounded Major Ormond was taken prisoner. He succumbed to his wounds in captivity on 10 November. His body was never returned.

That morning, as the survivors took stock and tended to 170 wounded, elements of the US 5th Cavalry tried to breach a CPVA roadblock south of Unsan to rescue the US3/8th Cavalry. The Chinese were positioned on a ridge near Turtle Head Bend on the Kuryong River. However, without the support of heavy artillery, the US 5th Cavalry failed in its attack at what became known as Bugle Hill,

Bitter cold, bitter fight. (Photo NARA)

suffering 350 casualties in the attempt. General Gay made the difficult decision to call off the rescue effort, effectively abandoning the 3rd Battalion.

As darkness fell and air support retired, the Chinese returned, launching six attacks with heavy-mortar fire in support. There was no let-up on 3 November, and at first light on the 4th, remnants of the battalion attempted to break out. First Lieutenant Walter Mayo recalls how 'We literally crawled over Chinese bodies, a carpet of them, for almost 100 yards.'[*]

According to the Army's Center for Military History in Washington, the US 1st Cavalry Division 'sustained 1,481 men killed, wounded or missing in action at Unsan. The US 8th Cavalry Regiment lost more than 1,000, mostly in the 3rd Battalion'.[†] The 3rd Battalion had ceased to exist as an organized force.

The sector boundary between US I Corps and the retiring ROKA II Corps crossed the Ch'ŏngch'ŏn River at Kunu-ri. On 3 November, the 5th Regimental Combat Team (5RCT), US 24th Division, took up a rear-guard position at the village to protect the withdrawing South Korean corps. The next morning, however, the CPVA broke through the ROKA lines, forcing the South Koreans to retreat through the 5RCT position.

To the north of the Ch'ŏngch'ŏn, the 19th Regiment, US 24th Division, facing imminent Chinese envelopment, fell back to the south bank, abandoning vehicles and equipment in the process. But a successful counterattack by elements of the 21st Regiment, US 24th Division, restored most of the 19th's positions north of the river.

As the rout at Unsan continued to unfold, the resultant confusion in the US Eighth Army chain of command prompted General Walker to immediately withdraw US I Corps to the south of the Ch'ŏngch'ŏn River. In conjunction with his now defensive dispositioning of resources, Walker rushed in units of the 19th Infantry Regiment, US 24th Division, and the 27th British Commonwealth Brigade (27th British) to the north bank to guard bridges and armour crossings over the river.

By 24 October, the 27th British had pushed north of the occupied North Korean capital, P'yŏngyang, arriving at Sinanju to cross the Ch'ŏngch'ŏn River. Over three days, the brigade had covered 55 miles, spearheading the UN advance north from P'yŏngyang. On their right, the ROKA 1st Division entered Anju.

At high tide in the morning—around 8.30—and employing thirty American assault boats, the 1st Battalion, Middlesex Regiment (1/Middlesex) started to cross to the north bank, securing high ground to the north of the bridges. At this time, brigade commander, Brigadier Basil Coad, received fresh orders to continue with his drive northward on Pakch'ŏn, 9 miles away, from where he was to swing east to Chŏngju, along the axis commonly referred to as the 'MacArthur Line'.

A bridge farther upriver toward Anju would have to be used for brigade vehicles to cross. A reconnaissance patrol from the 1st Battalion, Argyll and Sutherland Highlanders (1/Argylls) reported the route to Anju clear of enemy troops, with the town itself in ROKA hands.

---

* Mike Mokrzycki, *Los Angeles Times*, 1 May 1994.

† Ibid.

M16 MGMC
half-track.
(Photo US Army)

With the first United Nations contingent from Britain aboard, the Empress of Australia majestically entered the harbour of Pusan. Once again at the yard-arm proudly fluttered the pennant of the 45th Field Regiment, Royal Artillery.

Foot by foot the old lady edged her way to one of the trickiest berths of her career. The pilot seemed to know no English. The Captain certainly knew no Korean. The operation was fraught with peril.

On the quay an American negro band gave a spirited rendering of Anchors Aweigh which struck a somewhat incongruous note. For an encore they slipped into the rhythm of the deep South with the St. Louis Blues. A platoon of South Korean schoolgirls, armed with national flags of curious design, thrashed the air with commendable fervour. Gently we touched the pier. The Royal Regiment of Artillery had added one more country to its impressive record.

A cosmopolitan reception committee, complete with floral tributes, did the honours. This touching, if tedious, formality over, we were more than glad to find Brigadier [Thomas] Brodie and Major [Harry] Withers with details that filled in the gaps in our future.[*]

*   *Korean Episode: The Story of the 45th Field Regiment, Royal Artillery, in the Korean War*, WO308/44, National Archives, Kew.

On patrol: 3rd Battalion, The Royal Australian Regiment, British and Commonwealth 27th Brigade. (Photo Australian War Memorial)

The next morning—25 October—the 3rd Battalion, Royal Australian Regiment (3RAR), set off across the Ch'ŏngch'ŏn near Kujin, its objective to push up the road toward Pakch'ŏn and establish a beachhead to the west of the T'aeryong River.

Over the next two days, the Australians battled with two KPA companies to secure its objectives, sustaining thirty casualties.[*]

By 11 a.m. on 27 October, the whole 27th British had crossed the Taeryong, allowing the US 5RCT to pass through on their drive to T'aech'ŏn. Following behind, the 1/Argylls spearheaded Brigadier Coad's continued advance, all the while encountering stiff resistance from remnants of the KPA 17th Brigade. Described by Coad as 'the stiffest enemy opposition by the Brigade since the days of the Naktong River', on 29 October, the Australians suffered nine killed and twenty-nine wounded.[†]

On 31 October, at Chŏngju the 27th British enjoyed their first day of rest and refit since arriving in Korea. However, there was little to celebrate as brigade HQ received the news that the 3RAR commanding officer, Lieutenant-Colonel Charles H. Green had died of wounds received when enemy artillery had shelled the brigade's position the previous day.

---

[*] Gerry van Tonder, *Korean War Allied Surge: Pyongyang Falls, UN Sweep to the Yalu, October 1950* (Pen and Sword Military, Barnsley, 2019).

[†] *27th British Commonwealth Brigade War Diary September to October 1950* (Australia War Memorial Archives, Campbell).

Brigadier Coad concluded the month's report:

Elsewhere the news was good with advances continuing on all sides. Disquieting reports, however, about the presence of Chinese troops had been received from intelligence sources over the past few days and some PWs have already been taken.

Brigadier T. Brodie, Commander of 29 British Independent Group, visited the Brigade Commander and stayed the night at Bde, HQ.[*]

For Brigadier Coad, the impact of Chinese forces south of the Yalu was sudden and urgent, in the form of orders for a general withdrawal. The defeat of ROKA II Corps at the hands of the CPVA XXXVIII Corps, commanded by Liang Xing-chu, in the general area north of Tŏkch'on, had exposed the US I Corps' right flank. While the US 24th Division was pulled back to avoid being cut off and to shorten the line, on the afternoon of 1 November the 27th British HQ and 1/Argylls moved to Pakch'ŏn. Due to a shortage of American-supplied transport, 3RAR had to remain at Chŏngju and 1/Middlesex at T'aech'ŏn to await further orders.

The next day, 27th British was tasked with taking up defensive positions around T'aech'ŏn, where 1/Middlesex was already blocking the approaches from the north. General Walker then withdrew the US 5RCT from Kusŏng through T'aech'ŏn and the US 19RCT, who was at T'aech'ŏn, to a defensive position 10 miles south of the town. The US 21RCT was pulled back to Chŏngju.

By mid-afternoon, the 1/Argylls and 3RAR were finally transported back to T'aech'ŏn, the latter into brigade reserve, where Coad was to hold the town and its surrounds. However, at 3 p.m., warning orders were received for the brigade to be ready to move at short notice to Sukch'ŏn, south of the Ch'ŏngch'ŏn. It was Walker's intention for US 19RCT to form a bridgehead at Pakch'ŏn through which the 27th British would pass to divisional reserve at Sukch'ŏn. The river would then be held by US 5RCT on the left, US 21RCT in the centre, and US 1 Cavalry Division on the right. Only then would US 19RCT cross to the south bank into divisional reserve.

On 4 November, elements of the CPVA engaged the US 19RCT, infiltrating the rear of one of the battalions, who were forced to abandon vehicles and equipment as they hastily withdrew. Capturing Tŏkch'on, the CPVA XXXVIII Corps pushed west to threaten UN forces at Kunu-ri. The US 2nd Division was rushed up to stem the Chinese advance north-east of Kunu-ri, while US 1st Cavalry Division, less 8th Cavalry Regiment, took up positions to the west. To the east of the town, in the direction of Tŏkch'on, the ROKA II Corps, still in the process of reforming, set up defences.

At around 8 a.m. the following morning, the US 61st Field Artillery Battalion (61 FAB), in a line straddling the road 3,000 yards south of Pakch'ŏn, came under heavy enemy fire from hills to the right of their position. The Chinese penetrated the gun lines, forcing the

---

[*]   Ibid.

Under fire.
(Photo NARA)

After several hours of all-out fighting, a company from the 1st Argyll and Sutherland Highlanders, accompanied by American tanks, managed to battle its way down the road and enter our perimeter. An hour or so earlier at battalion, the Scottish commander had asked Major Fisher, "Can your chaps hold a bit longer?" Fisher replied, "I guess, by God, we can. We've been holding them for four hours." The next day we were told what happened next. The Argylls' senior NCO asked his CO, "Shall we attack in packs, sir?" The CO answered that the lads could remove their packs and put them by the side of the road. He added, "But see that they are aligned neatly."

GIs standing around watched in disbelief. Once the packs were placed along the road (definitely neatly), the Argylls advanced down the road as nonchalantly as if on morning police call.

When the tanks appeared on the road, the Chinese pulled back and disappeared. The Argylls moved in. The British commander reported the success of his mission to his headquarters. Standing nearby I heard what he told his Scottish radioman. The radio operator relayed the good news in a long string of unintelligible "burns" and "ochs."

Private First Class Jimmy Marks
A Battery/61st Field Artillery Battalion[*]

---

[*] Donald Knox, *The Korean War, Pusan to Chosin: An Oral History.* (Harcourt Brace & Co., Orlando, 1985).

Americans to defend themselves with small arms. The 1/Argylls were ordered back across the Ch'ŏngch'ŏn, where they cleared the American artillery lines of Chinese forces, holding a line to the east of the road.

Brigadier Coad now started receiving signals of major enemy movement from the north and north-east. Fearing Chinese envelopment, Coad turned around to fight his way clear. With close air support, strafing and bombing the enemy with rockets, cannon and napalm, at 2 p.m., 3RAR jumped off while the 1/Argylls held their ground. The 1/Middlesex was then passed through to clear the road southward and, by last light, Coad was once more facing north. The US 61 FAB crossed to the south bank where fresh positions were set up and guns registered.

In the darkness, the Chinese launched several attacks on a forward 3RAR company on the brigade's left, with each wave being initiated by whistles and bugle calls. The Australians held the road, and by midnight everything went quiet and the situation stabilized. Coad estimated that around 200 CPVA had been killed and a similar number wounded, at a cost to the brigade of ten killed and seventy wounded, most from the 3RAR.

As the sun rose on 6 November, the now familiar bugle calls caused the UN troops along General Walker's newly positioned defence lines to brace themselves for further violent Chinese attacks. But in the heavy silence of anticipation, the CPVA failed to appear.

Douglas AD Skyraiders in close air support. (Photo US Navy)

The Chinese commander-in-chief, Peng Dehuai, had been successful in the first offensive in Korea, pushing General MacArthur's forces back across the Ch'ŏngch'ŏn River. Not only had his armies exacted major, morale-destroying victories over the ROKA, but they had effectively and quickly cleared the Yalu border zone of UN troops.

In Tokyo, an annoyed MacArthur demanded answers of General Walker. The US Eighth Army commander no longer harboured any doubts that Chinese forces had crossed into North Korea in very large numbers, the cause of his stalled advance on the Yalu. On 5 November, Walker sent a signal to MacArthur:

> An ambush and surprise attack by fresh, well-organized and well-trained units, some of which were Chinese Communist Forces, began a sequence of events leading to a complete collapse and disintegration of ROK II Corps of three divisions. Contributing factors were intense, psychological fear of Chinese intervention and previous complacency and overconfidence in all ROK ranks.
>
> A regrouping of forces, an active defense, a build-up of supplies pending resumption of offensive and advance to the border ... plans have been made for resumption of the offensive employing all forces available to the Army to meet the new factor of organized Chinese Communist Forces.[*]

---

[*] James McGovern, *To the Yalu: From the Chinese Invasion of Korea to MacArthur's Dismissal* (William Morrow, New York, 1972).

3. AIR SUPERIORITY CHALLENGED

Peering out of the sparse sanctuary of my hole's inside:
My eye travelled along snatches of tracers,
Busy sewing seams along the edges of the night's darkness,
Looking for a carcass to bury their bright lights in.

'One Time Out of History's Calendar'
Ashley Cunningham-Boothe
Royal Northumberland Fusiliers[*]

Weeks before North Korea invaded the south, American intelligence suggested that the Korean People's Air Force (KPAF) comprised an air regiment of 1,500 crew, including 150 pilots. Washington estimated that the KPAF was equipped with thirty-five Yakovlev Yak-9 and Ilyushin Il-10 fighter aircraft, three twin-engine bombers, two twin-engine transports, and around thirty-five Japanese and Soviet trainers.

On 27 June, shortly after noon, five KPAF fighters arrived at 10,000 feet over Seoul. Within minutes, North American F-82 Twin Mustangs from the US 68th and 339th squadrons took on the Yaks, bringing down three and sending the remainder back home at full throttle. The second—and final—KPAF presence came later that afternoon, when eight Soviet-made Ilyushin Il-10 'Beast' ground-attack aircraft appeared over Kimp'o to attack US transports on the ground. It was, however, a mismatch, as four Lockheed F-80C Shooting Star jet fighters of the US 35th Fighter-Bomber Squadron descended on the hapless North Koreans, immediately shooting down four of their aircraft—the first USAF victories by jet fighters. The Fifth Air Force had stamped its authority over Seoul and no further KPAF aircraft returned for the rest of the evacuation mission from Seoul that day.

As part of MacArthur's show of strength, on the afternoon of the 28 June, the first US Boeing B-29 Superfortress heavy bombers were deployed. Four B-29s of the US 19th Bombardment Group, armed with demolition bombs, split up as they reached the operational area, to bomb, in pairs, the road and rail parallel routes that ran from Seoul to Kapyong and from Seoul to Ŭijŏngbu. The aircrews were instructed to bomb anything that they felt was warranted.

Later quoted as having stated, 'North Korea air, operating from nearby bases, has been savage in its attacks in the Suwŏn area,' MacArthur verbally authorized General George E. Stratemeyer to cross the 38th Parallel to attack North Korean airfields. Recognized as a skilled tactician with excellent man-management skills, Stratemeyer had

---

[*] Ashley Cunningham-Boothe and Peter Farrar, Eds., *British Forces in the Korean War* (British Korean Veterans Association, Halifax, 1997).

Above: Soviet Yak-9s, Second World War.

Below: A USAF Douglas B-26B Invader on a mission over North Korea, 1951. (Photo USAF)

been posted to Tokyo in April 1949 to assume command of the US Far East Air Force (FEAF). This comprised the Fifth Air Force in Japan, the Thirteenth Air Force in the Philippines, and the Twentieth Air Force in Okinawa. Stratemeyer would direct the first aerial attacks against the invading KPA forces as well as the evacuation of Americans from Seoul.

The US 8th Tactical Reconnaissance Squadron immediately capitalized on the new freedom by conducting photo-reconnaissance sorties over KPAF airfields north of the 38th. This mission facilitated the rapid—many argued overdue—deployment at of eighteen B-26s from the US 3rd Bombardment Group, their target the principal KPAF air base at the North Korean capital, P'yŏngyang.

At the same time, at Kobe in Japan, Marine fighter squadron VMF-214 'Black Sheep', US Marine Air Group 33, was preparing to embark on the USS *Sicily* (CVE-118) for operations in Korean waters. After two days of field carrier training at Itami Air Force Base, Japan, on 3 August the squadron's twenty-four gull-winged Chance Vought F4U Corsairs flew out to the *Sicily* which had been cruising in the Tsushima Straits. Four Corsairs from the USS *Badoeng Strait*, already overhead on a reconnaissance sortie, immediately set about strafing the invading KPA column at low level. Retaliatory North Korean groundfire hit two of these iconic gull-winged workhorses of the Pacific theatre, causing one to crash.

Shortly thereafter, a second wing of Corsairs and USAF F-51 Mustangs continued to wreak havoc on the sitting column of North Korean vehicles. The American aircraft

NO A-BOMBS FOR KOREA—TRUMAN

Still Hoping Fervently for World Peace
President Truman said in Washington yesterday that he was not considering the use of the atomic bomb in Korea. He said he was still hoping fervently for world peace. He hoped it would not be necessary to have an all-out mobilisation of the United States. Until there was an all-out mobilisation there would not be price controls, wage controls, or rationing.

He declined to comment when asked if he was still as hopeful for world peace as he was a few months ago. It was when a Pressman recalled that the President had once said that he would not hesitate to use the atomic bomb if needed in a case of aggression that Mr Truman replied very firmly that he was not considering it.

He also said he would ask Congress for more money to arm the free nations which are in danger of Communist aggression. It is understood that he will ask for up to 5,000,000,000 dollars (£1,785,000,000).

U.S. Will Call Up 100,000 Men
The U.S. Defence Department in Washington announced yesterday that 100,000 men will be called up for the Army during September and October. President Truman has signed an executive order extending for twelve months all enlistments in the armed services.

Aberdeen Press and Journal, 28 July 1950

Carrier-borne F4U Corsairs prepare for a sortie. (Photo US Navy)

carriers USS *Valley Forge, Bon Homme Richard* and *Essex* would also become synonymous with the early phases of the Korean War, when the Americans were being pushed ever south down the peninsula.

On the ground, US 25th Division commander, Major General William B. Kean, had positioned Tactical Air Control Parties (TACPs) close to the front, from where forward air controllers could, with precision, identify and pinpoint enemy targets. This 'live' information would immediately be conveyed to the rudimentary Tactical Air Control Center, established within the US 6132nd Tactical Air Control Group. Given the call sign 'Mellow Control', the radarless facility exercised control over all the TACPs in country, in addition to providing the JOC with a radio network. Mellow Control would then disseminate enemy target information to North American T-6 Texan forward air control aircraft of the recently activated US 6147th Tactical Control Squadron, Airborne, designated 'Mosquitos'. The success of air support provided in this manner was largely due the freedom of movement that the Texan aircraft enjoyed in the air.

Arguably, the US Far East Air Force (FEAF) made the biggest impact on the outcome of any phase of the Korean War in August 1950. By this time, the US Fifth Air Force had placed TACPs with each American and South Korean divisional, regimental and corps HQ. American fighter aircraft, flying from bases in Japan, would report in to the tactical air control centre at the rate of two every fifteen minutes to receive mission information and be directed to the relevant TACP. By 23 August, twenty-nine North American T-6 Texan 'Mosquitoes' of the US 6147th Tactical Air Control Group were providing dawn-to-dusk airborne tactical coordination. In August, FEAF flew 7,400 ground support sorties, up from 4,600 the previous month.

Commander of FEAF Bomber Command, Major General Emmett O'Donnell, expressed support for the proposed carpet bombing of North Korean military concentrations in the Naktong area. He was confident that effective saturation bombings with 500-pound bombs in a 3-square-mile target area could be achieved with available aircraft.

On 16 August, B-29 heavy bombers commenced a bombing sortie on an estimated 40,000 KPA troops, poised to strike at the US 1st Cavalry Division, in a 27-square-mile target area. For over thirty minutes, ninety-eight of these bombers, operating at between 5,000 and 10,000 feet, dropped 3,084 500-pound and 150 1,000-pound bombs over the designated target. Not since the D-Day Normandy invasion in June 1944 had this magnitude of air support for ground forces been conducted.

The successful amphibious landing at Inch'ŏn, the defence of and breakout from the Pusan Perimeter by the US Eighth Army, interdiction bombing of key strategic sites in North Korea, and the advance on the Yalu River would, arguably, not have taken place without the unchallenged tactical and strategic air supremacy that General MacArthur enjoyed in the first four months of the conflict.

FEAF B-29s on a bombing raid over the Korean Peninsula. (Photo NARA)

At the end of the Second World War and with the demise of the Japanese KwAndong Army in Manchuria, Chinese Communist Party leader Mao Zedong turned his attention to the development of an aviation arm in his fight against the Chinese Nationalists. In March 1946, the Northeast Aviation School was founded, with 660 personnel and forty Japanese aircraft. Captured Japanese pilots and groundcrew of the 26th Training Group, Japanese Second Air Army, under Major Hayasi Yuichiro were persuaded to stay in Manchuria at the core of the embryonic pilot school.

However, with limited resources, progress was slow. In the absence of trainer aircraft, the school had to contend with extremely poorly maintained Japanese Tachikawa Ki-55 Type 99 advanced trainers. The arrival at the aviation unit of Soviet-trained Chinese pilots in early 1947 would see the school adopt Soviet teaching techniques and materials.

By July 1949, the school had trained 126 pilots, 322 mechanics, 24 navigators and 88 supplementary groundcrew. A select handful of pilots underwent combat flight conversion training on Japanese Kakajima Ki-43 Hayabusa fighters, known to the Japanese as the 'Peregrine Falcon' and to the Allies as 'Oscar'.

Later that year, the birth of the People's Republic of China brought with it an entente with the Soviet Union, the new nation in the Asian communist fold amenable to Soviet Marxist-Leninist ideology and ripe for the Russians to assist with the foundation of the People's Liberation Army Air Force (PLAAF). Successfully learning to fly Soviet aircraft, these pioneering PLAAF pilots formed the first combat wings in May 1950. Commander of

Japanese Kakajima Ki-43 Hayabusa fighter.

the PLA XIV Corps, Liu Yalou, was tasked with organizing the new air force and to formalize requests for Soviet aid. The Central Military Commission (CMC) endorsed Liu's recommendations, allowing for the PLA XIV Corps HQ staff to be incorporated with the Aviation Bureau to form the air force command structure.

Then, after months of negotiations, in August 1949, Marshal Konstantin Vershinin, commander-in-chief of the Soviet air force informed the Communist Chinese delegation that the Soviet Union would train 350 to 400 pilots within a year, followed by conversion courses to Soviet-made aircraft and combat techniques. This would facilitate China establishing two fighter divisions and one bomber division. In addition, 878 Soviet personnel would be attached to PLAAF training schools in China: 100 at each fighter school, 120 at each bomber school and several at the PLAAF HQ.

In terms of hardware, Vershinin pledged 120 Lavochkin La-9 fighters, 40 Tupolev Tu-2 bombers, 4 Ilyushin Il-12 transports, and a total of 270 trainers, comprising Yakovlev Yak-18 and Yak-11, Lavochkin La-9UT and La-2UT aircraft. Beijing, while grateful for the opportunity granted by the Soviet Union to establish an air force, was unhappy about being charged new prices for old equipment.

By the time of the outbreak of the Korean War, China had established regional air offices in six military zones, in the characteristic Chinese dual command and operational structure of air and ground forces. Training schools and air stations proliferated, such that between 1949 and 1952, 13,000 army personnel from ground units had been selected to undergo flight training.

In June 1950, China established its first air unit, the 4th Mixed Aviation Brigade, at Nanjing in the east of the country. Made up of two fighter regiments, a bomber regiment and an attack regiment, the brigade was equipped with 155 aircraft: 38 Mikoyan-Gurevich MiG-15s, 39 Lavochkin La-11s, 39 Tupolev Tu-2s, 25 Ilyushin Il-10s and 14 trainers. By the end of 1953, the PLAAF had a strength of 290,000 personnel, with 4,500 aircraft, including 2,650 fighters.

From the moment Kim Il-sung sent his troops crashing across the 38th Parallel into an unsuspecting South Korea—and United States—Moscow and Beijing were reluctant to become militarily directly involved on the Korean Peninsula. Sixteen of Mao's armies had been posted to southern China in anticipation of an attack on Taiwan. Apart from agreeing to repatriate thousands of North Korean troops attached to the PLA, Mao displayed little concern for events in Korea, electing not to deploy extra troops on the Manchurian border.

In the Kremlin, however, Joseph Stalin was becoming increasingly anxious about China's ambivalent attitude to events on its border. The Soviet leader had no desire to enter into combat with American troops in Korea, so increased his pressure on Mao to deploy three armies to the Korean border. Beijing's response was, for Stalin, annoyingly tardy—in fact China was in 1950 working on reducing its standing army by 1.5 million soldiers. The Chinese reaction, eventually, was a request for Soviet air cover for the three Chinese armies already stationed in Manchuria.

The Soviet-made MiG-15. (Photo TDelCoro)

On 7 July, China's CMC met to discuss what military preparations should be made for the Korean War. The outcome was the formation of the Northeast Border Defence Army, into which was transferred nine divisions of the PLA XIII Corps to be deployed near the Korean border. However, Stalin was not privy to these decisions, and with the Americans now in full open combat with the North Korean invaders, on 13 July he pressured Beijing for a response. He reminded China that he had 124 aircraft on standby to provide air cover for the nine PLA divisions once on station. There was also an implication that Soviet pilots would remain in China long enough to train her pilots on MiG-15bis jet aircraft, and then leave the Soviet aircraft behind on their departure.

On 21 July, the Soviet 151st Guard Fighter Aviation Division (151st GIAD), under Major General Ivan Belov, received orders to fly to north-eastern China. Consisting of the 28th, 72nd and 139th Guards Fighter Aviation regiments (GIAP), prior to deployment all Soviet insignia and markings were removed. Upon arrival at the Mukden (72nd GIAP), Liaoyang (139th GIAP) and Anshan (28th GIAP) airfields, the Russian pilots were issued with Chinese uniforms and documentation.

By October, with American-led UN forces deep into North Korea, tensions in the region increased considerably as MacArthur neared the Yalu River. Moscow now had five motorized divisions ready for immediate deployment to Korea as it poured war matériel into China, including the new MiG-15 jet fighter. At this time, four Soviet Air Fighter Divisions (IADs), all equipped with MiG-15s, had arrived in China: the 57th, 126th, 137th and 180th GIAPs. Later in the month, a newly activated air division, the Soviet 50th IAD, was set up on the Liaodong Peninsula. Commanded by Colonel A.I. Khalutin, and made

W. ALLIES PLEDGE

Where Troops Will Halt

Mr. Younger, British Minister of State ... said that, while occupation of all Korea would not be continued any longer than necessary, it would be "cynical repudiation" of responsibility to let United Nations forces go home before their task was done.

Mr. Austin (U.S.) also advised Russia and Communist China that there was no need to fear aggression from General MacArthur's troops. "We want nothing from Korea," he said. "We want no bases there. We don't want to and will not threaten any other country through "temporary presence of American troops in Korea on a United Nations mission. The United States will cooperate in fulfilling the policy of this resolution that United forces will remain in Korea only so long as is necessary for achieving the essential objectives of the General Assembly—the establishment of a unified independent and democratic Government of Korea. After the end of fighting the quicker Korea is permitted to live its own life without foreign interference the better."

Belfast Telegraph, 7 October 1950

up of experienced pilots flying MiG-15s, the IAD was formed to specifically conduct combat missions over Korea.

Through November and December, eleven Soviet air divisions arrived in China, where they were grouped under the Soviet 67th Aviation Group, commanded by Colonel General Stepan Krasovsky. It was made clear to the Second World War 'Hero of the Soviet Union' that his responsibilities would be limited to expand the PLAAF's air capabilities as quickly as possible, before handing over all their aircraft and equipment to the Chinese and returning home.

As October drew to a close, Soviet pilots of the 151st GIAD, flying MiG-15s, conducted patrols along the Yalu, complying with orders not to violate the border or engage UN aircraft in combat. Sorties generally covered the western end of the Yalu where the river disgorges into the Yellow Sea. On one side of the river, the Chinese city of Andong faced Sinŭiju on the Korean south bank, both centres of strategic importance to the respective countries.

With the North Korean air force effectively destroyed in the first few months of the conflict, and as the CPVA forced MacArthur back, commander of FEAF General George E. Stratemeyer announced with confidence his ability to maintain air supremacy, provide close air support and to fulfil its logistical obligations to ground forces. There was, however, internal debate as to the comparative efficacy of the conventional F-51 Mustangs and F-4U Corsairs against the F-80 Shooting Stars.

North Korean MiG-15 pilot
Lieutenant No Kum-Sok.

On the afternoon of 1 November 1950, Soviet fighters resolved the issue for the Americans. Hopelessly outclassed, startled USAF Mustang pilots 'hit the deck' and scarpered as the latest Russian swept-back-wing fighter jets flashed past them. First put on public display at Moscow's Tushino Airport on Soviet Aviation Day in February 1948, the Mikoyan-Gurevich prototype I-310, developed as Product S, was given the service designation MiG-15. Generating 5,000 pounds' thrust, the original engine was a Soviet copy of the Rolls-Royce B.41 Nene. Shortly after the Second World War, Rolls-Royce sold fifteen Nene engines to the Soviet Union, with a caveat that they would not be used for military purposes. As tensions between the West and Moscow escalated to dangerous levels during the Berlin crisis in 1948, the Soviet Union reneged on the commercial contract with Rolls-Royce, developing through reverse engineering the Klimov RD-45 and VK-1 engines for fitting to the new MiG-15. The upgraded MiG-15bis variant was used during the Korean War.

During this period, the Chinese actively bolstered its air defences at Andong. In quick time, a 6,000-feet concrete runway was laid down. Early-warning radar, with a 150-mile range—extending well into North Korea—was installed.

Further undermining General MacArthur's dominance in the air, early in November the Soviets activated the 28th IAD. Commanded by Second World War fighter ace Colonel A.V. Aleyukhin, the new division comprised the 67th and 139th IAPs from the Soviet 151st

A MiG-15 getting hit over Korea. (Photo USAF)

GIAD. The latter retained the 28th IAP and the 72nd GIAP, with new commander Colonel A.Y. Sapozhnikov. Each division was equipped with sixty-two MiG-15s. On paper, the two air divisions were to adhere to their brief of training Chinese pilots and handing over the aircraft to the PLAAF. However, the events over the Yalu on 1 November signalled the start of two and a half years of Soviet air combat in Korea.

Official USAF records give 8 November 1950 as aviation's first aerial combat engagement between jet aircraft, with Lieutenant Russell Brown of the US 51st Fighter-Interceptor Wing receiving the credit for shooting down the first MiG of the war.[*]

However, claims and counter-claims still dominate the historic event, with the Russians contending that, on 1 November, Lieutenant Semyen Khomich of the Soviet 72nd GIAP was the first jet pilot to bring down another jet fighter. The USAF admitted to the loss of an F-80 on that day, but as a result of anti-aircraft fire from the Chinese side of the Yalu. Both belligerents agree that US Navy pilot William Amen shot down Soviet Senior Lieutenant Mikhail Grachev's MiG-15 on 9 November.

At this time, General Belov and General Krasovsky met with PLAAF commander Liu Yalou at Shenyang to discuss ways in which the Soviet Union could assist with the defence of north-east China. Arising out of this meeting, on 15 November Stalin ordered

---

[*]   Robert Frank Futrell, *The United States Air Force in Korea, 1950–1953* (Progressive Management, 1983)

the formation of the 64th Fighter Air Corps (IAK) to command the two MiG-15 divisions on 'special duties' in China. Based in Shenyang, Belov was appointed to command the corps.

To deter Chinese troops from crossing the Yalu River, on 6 November the Pentagon, under immense pressure from MacArthur via the Joint Chiefs of Staff (JCS), authorized the FEAF Bomber Command to use whatever means at its disposal to destroy the Yalu bridges along the Korean border with Manchuria. Two days after receiving their orders, FEAF despatched seventy B-29 heavy bombers on a mission to firebomb Sinŭiju, and a further nine to bomb the two Yalu bridges at that point. MiGs from the two divisions at Shenyang and An-Tung executed fifty sorties, but the distances from refuelling facilities saw the Soviet fighters fail to bring down a single American bomber. The raid virtually levelled the city of Sinŭiju, killing 2,000 civilians.

The Soviets flew 160 sorties from 8 to 10 November, but with very limited success against UN aircraft. Fuel was a major inhibiting factor. Drop tanks were in short supply, which meant that flying time was restricted to only one hour. The situation was compounded by inexperienced Ground Control Interceptor (GCI) operators failing to direct the MiGs into visual contact with UN aircraft. As a result, UN propeller-driven and slow jet aircraft continued to enjoy relative freedom of movement along the Yalu.

The unsatisfactory scenario placed the Kremlin in a quandary. Not only were they falling short of their promises to militarily assist a fellow communist state, but the reputation of their rapidly growing Cold War air arm was being tarnished. For Stalin, the only face-saving solution would be to transfer his most experienced air combat regiments to Korea, while simultaneously relieving the 151st GIAD and 28th IAD of their combat duties to concentrate fully on the training of Chinese pilots. The Soviets committed a further 120 MiG-15s to Belov's 64th IAK, while placing the Soviet 50th IAD at the Russian Sanshilibao Air Base on the Liaodong Peninsula on a state of immediate readiness to move.

Commanded by a Hero of the Great Patriotic War, Colonel A.V. Pashkevich, the Soviet 50th IAD comprised the 29th GIAP, having just completed a mission to Shanghai, and the 177th IAP, equipped with the powerful MiG-15bis. On 20 November, the unit flew to Anshan, from where they would defend Andong and Sinŭiju, and the international bridges connecting the two cities. There would be no responsibility for the training of Chinese pilots, but a combative support role in the Korean War.

In Washington, despite the fact that China had hitherto not challenged UN forces in the skies over North Korea, US Chief of Staff of the Air Force, Lieutenant General Hoyt S. Vandenberg, became increasingly anxious that the US Fifth Air Force in Korea lacked comparable modern jet fighters with which to counter the threat of MiG-15s from north of the Yalu. With the proviso that forward airfields be made available near combat areas, General Stratemeyer and General Earle E. Partridge, commander of the US Fifth Air Force, snapped up Vandenberg's offer of a wing each of Republic F-84E Thunderjet fighter-bombers and North American F-86A Sabre jet fighters. Within a fortnight,

The USAF bombs the international bridges across the Yalu River at Sinŭiju. (Photo USAF)

the US 27th Fighter-Escort Wing (US 27th Wing) and the US 4th Fighter-Interceptor Wing (US 4th Wing) had been deck-loaded on to carriers and dispatched to Japan.

General Partridge had initially intended to place the combat element of the US 4th Wing and their Sabres at occupied P'yŏngyang, and the US 27th Wing, Flying Thunderjets, at Kimp'o near Seoul. However, by the time the two wings were ready for combat deployment in early December, this was no longer possible. Leaving the US 27th Wing's rear echelon in Japan, the unit's Thunderjets were placed at Taegu Airfield, from where they adopted an armed reconnaissance and close-support role. The wing conducted its first mission on 6 December.

The US 4th Wing was instead diverted to an already congested Kimp'o, where only some of the wing, mainly Sabres of the US 336 Fighter-Interceptor Squadron, could be accommodated.

Essentially adopting the Luftwaffe's swept-wing design of the Messerschmitt Me 262, the North American Aviation Company fitted the F-86 with a J-47-GE-13 engine, with a thrust of 5,200 pounds. The Sabre was not supersonic and, even with two external 120-gallon wing tanks, only had a combat range of 490 miles.

CHINESE REDS POUR OVER FRONTIER TO AID NORTH KOREANS

Tokyo, Tuesday
Gen. MacArthur's spokesman said that, according to. the North Korean radio, 25,000 Chinese had crossed the border to "participate in a patriotic demonstration" in Korea. The broadcast added that another 3,000 were on the way. Peking Communist radio said 3,000 Chinese were fighting with the North Koreans and that a further 10,000 volunteers were assembled north of the Yalu River. Gen. MacArthur's spokesman, reporting a steady stream of Chinese men and material crossing the river, said that Chinese troops had been met in positions consistent with Peking's declared plan to keep the rivers and power plants out of United Nations hands.

Air Battle
Soviet jet fighters turned and fled when challenged by United States Mustangs in the biggest aerial dogfight of the Korean war, cables Richard Hughes, Western Mail special correspondent. In a running fight near the Manchurian border 16 United States propeller-driven fighters clashed with 15 of the Reds' latest sweptback M.I.G. jets. No American aircraft were damaged. One Soviet aeroplane was shot down and three others damaged.

Skilful "Red" Pilots
United States pilots reported that the enemy pilots were most skilful and far superior to the pilots of the Yak fighters they had previously encountered. However, when the pressure was tough the Soviet aeroplanes took refuge in what Gen. MacArthur has satirically called the "privileged sanctuary" of Manchuria. As United States jets arrived the Soviet jets dived helter skelter for safety.

Western Mail, 8 November 1950

On 17 December, the wing undertook its first combat air patrol over the Yalu, led by Lieutenant Colonel Bruce H. Hinton, commander of the US 336 Fighter-Interceptor Squadron. The element, or flight, entered the Yalu combat zone at a sedate, fuel-saving 0.62 Mach, a deliberate tactic because of the distance from Kimp'o, but one which may have ended in disaster had the Americans encountered more skilled adversaries. Mid-afternoon a formation of four MiG-15s was spotted, but the Sabres were flying too slowly to effectively engage the Russians.

Fortunately, the MiGs had also located the American aircraft. Mistaking them for the slow F-80, the MiGs started to climb toward their enemy. Capitalizing on the good fortune,

F-84E Thunderjet fighters en route to Japan aboard the escort carrier USS *Sitkoh Bay* (CVE-86), August 1951. (Photo USAF)

the Sabres dived to gain the necessary speed to take on the MiGs. Not expecting to be challenged, the Russian pilots were taken by surprise, forcing them to dive and head for the Yalu. Colonel Hinton singled out the MiG formation number-two man and clung to his tail, from where he fired three long bursts from his four .50-calibre machine guns.

The MiG, in flames, spun to the ground and crashed. Hinton was credited with being the first Sabre pilot to achieve a kill in air-to-air combat against a MiG-15.

Over the next few days the Sabre pilots adhered to flying speeds that conserved precious fuel. The MiG pilots quickly recognized the Americans' tactics, hanging back at a safe distance until their opponents' time in the combat zone was about to end. They would then drop down on the Sabres at maximum speed, leaving the latter with insufficient time to both gain speed and engage the MiGs.

After 19 December, the Americans started to enter the combat zone at nothing below 0.85 Mach. This reduced available time to twenty minutes in which to patrol and fight if MiGs were encountered. At the same time, the strength of a Sabre patrol element was standardized at sixteen aircraft, consisting of four flights of four aircraft, arriving at five-minute intervals and at varying altitude.

The new tactics paid dividends on 22 December when two Sabre flights encountered fifteen MiGs. Led by US 4th Wing commander, Lieutenant Colonel John C. Meyer, for twenty minutes dogfights took place between treetop level and 30,000 feet. Six MiGs were accounted for, while, in an earlier dogfight, the Americans lost Captain Lawrence V. Bach when his Sabre was hit by MiG cannon fire. Bach ejected successfully, but was taken prisoner and interrogated by the Russians.

F-86E Sabre fighters over Korea. (Photo USAF)

Fifteen MiG-15s from the 1st Squadron, Soviet 177th IAP, led by squadron leader Captain Mikhailov, were on high altitude patrol when, at 11.25 a.m. they spotted a flight of Sabres over Yŏmju train station. Captain Niklay Vorobyov would later describe what had happened:

> I was first to spot the enemy, flying in a diamond formation at 12,000m (39,000 feet). I went after them while the rest of our group fell behind. I leveled off behind the trailing Sabre and closed in to about 100m from its starboard side. I fired a burst that went high, then a second burst that went low. The Sabre started banking right and I followed him. My third burst went to his right, and the fourth burst hit him when he flew into it; I must have been no more than 80 meters away. One 37mm cannon shell went into the tail pipe. Debris and wreckage sailed past me as the enemy plane caught fire and fell away. I radioed "One down! Falling down! On fire!" The three other Sabres broke and dived away. When my gun camera film was developed later, I was told by flight instructor Safronov, "I've never seen pictures with such close-ups of the enemy aircraft."[*]

Until the end of December, the US 4th Wing adequately demonstrated that it was able to efficiently patrol the Yalu and deter or destroy the fastest known communist fighter jet. The element had conducted 234 sorties during the month, which saw 76 Sabres engage MiGs, resulting in eight kills, two probable kills and damage to another seven. The four-flights-of-four entry into the combat patrol zone—dubbed the 'jet stream'—proved successful, as the first flight to sight the enemy would call the other aircraft to his location for a combined attack. The 'fluid-four' flight configuration, in fingertip formation, was considered optimum.

However, after two weeks of combat, there was a consensus of opinion among pilots of the US 4th Wing that they had never before encountered such difficult combat situations. The Russians enjoyed a significant advantage by operating close to their base at Andong, allowing them to pick and choose the time and place to take on the Americans. Dogfights took place at near-supersonic speeds, making deflection shooting (shooting ahead of a moving target so that the target and projectile will meet) virtually impossible. This meant that the way to kill was to lock onto an opponent's tail and fire up his tailpipe. But opportunities for this were scarce.

Comparing the two aircraft, the Sabre pilots believed that they were matched in speed. The MiG-15 displayed superior climb and zoom attributes, but at low altitude and level flight, the Sabre had the edge. In terms of armament, the Sabre enjoyed an advantage over the mixed-calibre—two 23mm and one 37mm—low-cyclic rate of fire of the MiG's weaponry. However, the American airmen were disappointed with their kill rate,

---

[*] Thomas McKelvey Cleaver, *MiG Alley: The US Air Force in Korea 1950–53.* (Bloomsbury, Oxford, 2019)

saying that too many damaged MiGs remained airborne and were thus able to return to base. It was felt that heavier-calibre weapons, but with the same rate of fire as their .50-calibre guns, would sufficiently address this shortcoming. Added to this, the old Mk 18 (British-made Mk II Gyro) gunsights fitted to the Sabre were stiff and inconsistent. Perhaps radar-ranging gunsights would increase kill options available to the pilot.

All the while, Beijing appealed for Soviet air support for its ground operations. In late November, Peng Dehuai was preparing thirty CPVA divisions to launch a second offensive against the UN forces in North Korea. However, and despite the additional deployment of

RUSSIANS "READY AND ABLE" TO FIGHT

Soviet Marshal accuses U.S. of aggression
Accusing the United States of imperialism and armed aggression in Korea, the Soviet Deputy Prime Minister, Marshal Bulganin, said in a broadcast yesterday: "The Soviet people are ready and able to defend the interests of their fatherland, if necessary, with arms in their hands."

Marshal Bulganin was giving what is traditionally Russia's most important pronouncement of the year—the annual report delivered on the eve of the Revolution anniversary. He spoke to representatives of Moscow professional, political and army organisations at the Bolshoi Theatre In Moscow.

"Camp of peace"
"Under the leadership of the Communist Party of China, led by Comrade Mao Tse Tung, the great Chinese people is fighting actively for the cause of peace," he declared.

"United States imperialists are following a policy of instigating a new war and using the present circumstances to capture sources of raw materials and markets.

"The people's democracies, together with the German Democratic Republic, which firmly stands on a peace basis, and the heroic Korean people, which is fighting for its independence, liberty and peace, all these people constitute the camp of democracy, socialism and peace.

"The American Imperialists have now passed from a policy preparation of aggression to direct acts of aggression, the most blatant example being the armed intervention in Korea.

"The Soviet Government insisted from the beginning on peaceful settlement and proposed the withdrawal of all foreign troops from Korea, but the American Government, bent on a course of aggression, rejected all the Soviet proposals.

Belfast News-Letter, 7 November 1950

the Soviet 64th IAK, Soviet air involvement was restricted to a 30-mile radius of Andong. As a consequence, not only did Chinese ground operations lack the advantage of air support, but FEAF continued to attack CPVA supply lines while also providing the UN ground forces with essential assistance from the air.

Within days of launching his newest offensive, Peng complained to Beijing about logistical failures depriving his troops of ammunition and food as American bombers conducted uninterrupted interdiction raids on the North Korean transport infrastructure. On 23 December, a desperate Peng called on Mao to commit Chinese and North Korean air force units to the defence of supply lines south of P'yŏngyang and Wŏnsan once the respective airfields had been repaired. This would leave the Soviet air divisions responsible only for the Yalu–Taedong river axis.

This dovetailed well with Soviet thinking at the time. Moscow was increasingly convinced that General MacArthur had no intention of escalating the confrontation in North Korea. There would be no increase in the Soviet's air commitment, largely confirmed on 17 January 1951 when the first deputy of the chief of staff, Colonel General Sergey Shtemenko, instructed the Soviet air element in China to adopt a defensive role against UN forces. As the CPVA forced the American fighter-interceptor element from its North Korean bases, the Soviets gained air supremacy over 'MiG Alley'. Without sufficient escorts for its heavy bombers, FEAF Bomber Command was forced to stay clear of north-west Korea.

Possibly in recognition of the CPVA's ground offensives pushing MacArthur ever south, in April 1951 Stalin yielded to China's pressure by committing his most elite air units in support of the CPVA: the 324th and 303rd IADs.

Since mid-October 1950 when China crossed into North Korea, Beijing had poured substantial resources into turning the PLAAF into a combat-fit air force. The CPVA had to contend with an enemy who possessed more than 1,100 combat aircraft based on land and on offshore carriers. The bulk of USAF pilots had Second World War combat experience, having racked up in excess of 1,000 flying hours. Their Chinese adversaries, however, only had around 200 combat aircraft, with its pilots having accrued fewer than 100 hours' flying time. The MiG-15 pilots had only recently gone solo. None of the PLAAF pilots had combat experience.

Pragmatically, the Chinese knew they could not match the Americans in the air, adopting instead a strategy of avoiding air combat. A unit with up to 150 aircraft would be trained and be on standby for mobilization at short notice for timely attacks on American targets. To this end, four air regiments, comprising 120 MiG-15s, would be made available for supply-line protection in January and February 1951. Ambitiously, it was intended that by mid-April there would be six fighter regiments, two attack-aircraft regiments and four bomber regiments—360 aircraft—available for commitment to the war. On 4 December, Mao endorsed a plan for the PLAAF to give priority to the provision of air support to Peng's troops on the ground.

On 4 November, commander of the PLAAF units in China's South-Central Military Region, Liu Zhen, was transferred to assume command of the Northeast Military region,

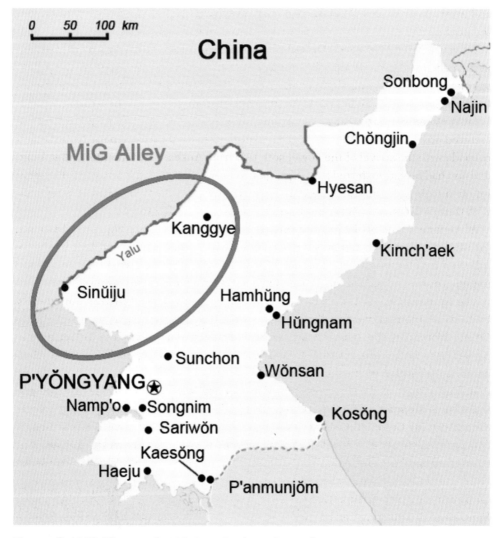

The so-called MiG Alley over the Yalu River border with Manchuria.

where he was tasked with organizing the CPVA Air Force. As with the whole of the PLAAF, Liu Zhen's command lacked essential aviation experience and skills. Staff was drawn from various military regions, and Moscow was approached once more for advisers. Stalin complied by sending a team led by Major General D. Golunov, but remained adamant that Moscow would not enter into a joint command with the PLAAF for the provision of air support in Korea.

China now turned to North Korean leader Kim Il-sung to form a joint air army command, who snapped up the offer. On 15 March, the CPVA–KPA joint command was formally established at Andong. Deputy commander of the PLAAF, Chang Qiankun, and commander of the KPA air force, Wang Yong, were appointed deputy commanders of the joint air force.

However, it would be several months before the whole new structure became effective. Of immediate concern for the PLAAF was its pilots' lack of combat experience, especially against the honed flying skills of the Americans. Without hands-on experience, the Chinese pilots would not be able to become a determining factor in the air war.

On 4 December 1950, Fang Ziyi, commander of the PLAAF 4th Aviation Division, received orders to move the 28th Flying Group, 10th Aviation Regiment, to Andong, to coincide with the arrival of the Soviet 50th IAD from Anshan. Two months earlier, Fang's division had been transferred from Shanghai to Liaoyang, where the unit was reorganized into two regiments: the 10th and 12th. Soviet commander Belov supplied each regiment with thirty MiG-15s, which were split equally into three flight groups.

At Andong, a Sino-Soviet joint air command was formed with the objective of exposing the Chinese pilots, who had only amassed twenty flying hours, to operational conditions followed by blooding in air combat. The greenhorn Chinese airmen would conduct missions during periods of low UN air activity, and at all times with Soviet cover.

The first such mission occurred on 28 December as a Chinese flight, commanded by Li Han, accompanied two Soviet flights over the Anju area, near the mouth of the Ch'ŏngch'ŏn River. The language barrier between the two nationalities was, however, an immediate—and in the future—communications shortcoming during combat. There could be no solution to this dilemma.

In January 1951, as the USAF was forced to abandon Kimp'o and Suwŏn under pressure from the unstoppable CPVA offensive, the PLAAF 29th and 30th flying groups joined the 28th Flying Group at Andong. On the 21st, having conducted seven uneventful combat missions, six MiGs of the PLAAF 28th combined with eight Soviet MiGs to intercept UN fighter-bombers over Anju. The Chinese flight engaged four USAF F-84 Thunderjets that were attacking the Ch'ŏngch'ŏn River bridge. Li Han reported damaging one of the American fighter-bombers, a claim substantiated by the Soviet pilots. A week later, Li Han claimed their first kill when he brought down a USAF F-80 over the Yellow Sea off the North Korean west coast. FEAF recorded the loss of a Shooting Star on that day.

With the objective of exposing more of its pilots to combat missions, in the first week

MiG destroyed over Korea. (Photo USAF)

of February the PLAAF replaced the 10th Aviation Regiment at Andong with the 12th Aviation Regiment. Pilots of the latter, having just completed basic combat training, had only logged fifteen flying hours in MiG-15s. Throwing pilots new to jet aircraft into a war situation would have costly consequences.

Early on 10 February, at Andong eight Soviet MiGs were scrambled when their radar detected incoming enemy aircraft. Chinese pilots joined the urgency of the moment, but inexperience and the language issue would result in two Chinese MiGs colliding as they left the runway. As it transpired, the aircraft were in fact a returning Chinese flight. A third MiG crashed after running out of fuel. A fortnight later, the PLAAF 12th Air Regiment was returned to Liaoyang.

In the second half of February, the Soviet 151st GIAD claimed shooting down twelve UN aircraft: six fighter-bombers and six heavy bombers. On the other hand, the Chinese had encountered the enemy on only 24 of its 145 combat missions during the same period. In terms of results, the Chinese claimed only one kill and damage to two others, for the loss of two MiGs.

Notwithstanding the exigencies of Chinese ground operations against UN forces in North Korea, Beijing now accepted that her MiG pilots would have to receive further intensive training for them to become meaningful contributors to the war in Korea. It would not be before the summer that the PLAAF's capabilities would be tested in combat once more. MiG Alley operations reverted as the sole responsibility of the Soviets.

4. A DARK THANKSGIVING

Then, from my raw-ragged sleep, to stark-naked awakeness –
Mortar bombs ripped vulgar clutches from the earth's bone-dry crust,
And arms and legs – I wondered who had "bought it,"
In my instant-packaged hell,
As all around me cries of wounded Fusiliers gnawed away at the edges of my sanity.

One Time Out of History's Calendar'
Ashley Cunningham-Boothe
Royal Northumberland Fusiliers[*]

With the sudden withdrawal of the CPVA at the conclusion of its first offensive, General MacArthur started to edge his forces back northward. Fuelled by the euphoria of strategic successes over the fleeing North Korean armies at Inch'ŏn and Wŏnsan, and the US Eighth Army's breakout from the beleaguered Pusan Perimeter, the vainglorious supreme commander of UN forces in Korea believed that the North Koreans would only be completely neutralized when the Yalu River was reached. On a fleeting visit in late November to north-west Korea from Tokyo, at Sinŭiju MacArthur was reported to have told his officers, 'Tell the boys that when they reach the Yalu they are going home. I want to make good my statement that they are going to eat Christmas dinner at home.'[†]

In the United States, where anti-communist rhetoric and propaganda were widespread, many worshipped MacArthur in almost 'Boys' Own' adoration, a heroic fighter on a crusade to defend the West from the evils of Moscow and Beijing. For MacArthur, the capture of P'yongyang and the drive to the Yalu would surpass his legendary Second World War 'return' to the Philippines, immortalized in the tale and double-life-sized bronze statues of the general wading ashore at Leyte. Was his interpretation of a threat from 300,000 fired-up Chinese troops deliberately misread? Could he continue to prosecute the war from the comfort of his Tokyo office? Was his rational judgement clouded by his quest for the ultimate military glory of his career in uniform? Such questions remain at the centre of the ongoing debate over MacArthur: hero or villain?

It had also been MacArthur's tactical but ill-conceived decision to split his UN forces into two independent commands: the US Eighth Army under Lieutenant General Walton H. Walker in the west and Major General Edward 'Ned' M. Almond in the east of the peninsula. A mountainous, inhospitable and trackless 75-mile-wide gap separated the two command sectors.

---

[*]   Ashley Cunningham-Boothe and Peter Farrar, Eds., *British Forces in the Korean War* (British Korean Veterans Association, Halifax, 1997).

[†]   *The Scotsman*, 25 November 1950.

General Douglas MacArthur.
(Photo NARA)

On 6 November, General Walker messaged an impatient MacArthur:

A regrouping of forces, an active defence, a build-up of supplies pending resumption of the offensive and advance to the border. Plans have been made for resumption of the offensive employing all forces available to the Army to meet the new factor of organized Chinese Communist Forces.[*]

On 1 November, the US 1st Marine Division jumped off from the east coast port of Hŭngnam to Yudam-ni on the western reaches of the Changjin, or Chosin, Reservoir. The commonly used name 'Chosin' is derived from the Japanese pronunciation. Upon covering the 80 miles to the reservoir, a major source of hydroelectric power for Manchuria, the Marines would strike toward the Yalu. Along the eastern seaboard, General Almond ordered the accomplished ROKA Capital Division to move on the far north-eastern corner of North Korea on the Soviet Siberian border. About 40 miles off the South Koreans' left flank, the US 7th Division was sent up a steep and narrow track toward the border town of Hyesanjin.

---

[*] James McGovern, *To the Yalu: From the Chinese Invasion of Korea to MacArthur's Dismissal* (William Morrow, New York, 1972).

U. S. CASUALTIES 29, 996

Washington, Friday
Official figures of American casualties in Korea rose to 29, 996 to-day—1,115 more than a week ago.
Of the total, there were 4,993 dead, 20,568 wounded, 4,439 missing in action.
The Army had 25,677 casualties, Navy 320, Marines 3,756, and the Air Force 243.
The Scotsman, 25 November 1950

Marine divisional commander, 57-year-old Major General Oliver P. 'The Professor' Smith had every reason to believe that his troops would encounter Communist Chinese soldiers, the latter having engaged the South Korean units that had reached the Changjin Reservoir on 29 October. The highly decorated Second World War combat veteran, who would in a short space of time famously comment, "Retreat, hell! We're not retreating, we're just advancing in a different direction," availed himself of the latest intelligence reports, which declined to accept full-scale Chinese intervention. If Smith had any misgivings, he kept them private.

Albeit in an informal briefing with his officers and staff at Hŭngnam, Colonel Homer Litzenberg, commander of the 7th Regiment, US 1st Marine Division (US 7th Marines), that would spearhead the division's move, was less reticent about what lay ahead of his men: 'We can expect to meet Chinese Communist troops, and it is important that we win the first battle. The results of that action will reverberate around the world, and we want to make sure that the outcome has an adverse effect in Moscow as well as Peking.'*

Harbouring at the village of Sudong-ni on the night of 2 November, just before midnight the US 7th Marines was attacked by an estimated 10,000 soldiers of the CPVA 124th Division. Through superior retaliatory fire and with the assistance of US 1st Marine Air Wing support, the Chinese were repelled. Three days later, the Marines were engaged in another vicious firefight at a Chinese roadblock on the track to the reservoir. Once more the Americans cleared the route and continued their advance into the mountains in the direction of Chinhŭng-ni. From here, the Marines struck directly north on Koto-ri. The track rose steeply as it wound its way through more than 10 miles of the hazardous Hwangch'oryŏng Pass, a sheer cliff face on one side and a yawning chasm on the other.

On 3 November, the main contingent of the British 29th Independent Infantry Brigade (British 29th), commanded by Major-General Thomas Brodie, had arrived at Pusan on board the 21,000-ton *Empress of Australia*. Reformed in September 1949, the brigade, with a strength of 7,500, was re-mustered after the outbreak of the Korean War as a member of

---

* Ibid.

Corpsmen of the US 1st Marine Division engage elements of the CPVA. (Photo USMC)

UN forces. The brigade comprised the 1st Battalion, Royal Northumberland Fusiliers; the 1st Battalion, the Gloucestershire Regiment (Glosters); the 1st Battalion, the Royal Ulster Rifles; C Squadron, 8th King's Royal Irish Hussars; C Squadron, 7th Royal Tank Regiment; 45 Field Regiment, Royal Artillery; 11 Light Anti-aircraft Battery, Royal Artillery and 170 Mortar Battery, Royal Artillery.

Almost immediately, the unit began its four-day train journey to its concentration area at Suwon, 20 miles south of Seoul. By 22 November, the British 29th, equipped with the new 52-ton Mk 3 Centurion main battle tank, reached Kaesong, 35 miles north-west of Seoul. The brigade still had 120 miles to cover to reach the north-western front, where it would come under the US I Corps command.

On 10 November, British special forces in the form of 41 (Independent) Commando, Royal Marines, joined the UN advance in North Korea. Commanded by Lieutenant-Colonel Douglas B. Drysdale, the 219 Royal Marine volunteers underwent intensive training at the Bickleigh Commando School before travelling to Japan in civilian clothes. They were issued with American winter uniforms and weapons—retaining their green berets and battle dress—and attached to the US Marine Corps.

At first light on 7 November, it became evident that the Chinese had broken off their contact and had mysteriously withdrawn. With the conclusion of his first offensive,

The Korean Peninsula

Siping

Huadian

Tumen

Vladivostok

USSI

China

Shenyang

Tonghua

Ji'an

Anshan

M a n c h u r i a

Tunien River

Ch'ongjin

Najin

Manp'o

Kanggye

Yalu River

Kimch'aek

Dandong

Kusong

Yŏngbyon

North Korea

Hamhung

Sea of Japan

Korea Bay

P'yŏngyang

Wŏnsan

Namp'ŏ

Injin River

P'yŏnggyang

Haeju

38°

Ongjin

Kangnŭng

Inchon

Seoul

Samch'ŏk

Wŏnju

Ch'ŏnan

Ham River

Chŏnju

Yellow Sea

Taejŏn

Naktong River

Andong

Kunsan

P'ohang

South Korea

Taegu

Korea Strait

Masan

Uisan

Pusan

Mokp'o

Kŏje-do

Hiroshin

Yŏsu

Tsushima

Cheju

Ashiya air base

Kitakyushu

Fukuoka

Chin-do

Japan

Itazuke air base

Cheju-do

Sasebo

DUDLEY WALL - 2017

Above and below: An American M4A3E8 Sherman tank (top) and a Soviet-made T34/85 tank. (Photos Gary Todd and Jozef Kotulič)

A Chinese/North Korean propaganda poster of the Korean War.

Above and below: Restored MiG-15 and F-86F Sabre jet fighters (top) and Republic F-84 Thunderjet fighters. (Photos Tim Felce and USAF)

Mao's peasant soldiers.

Above and below: American Willys MB jeep (top) and a Soviet GAZ-67. (Photos Gerry van Tonder and Vanzan)

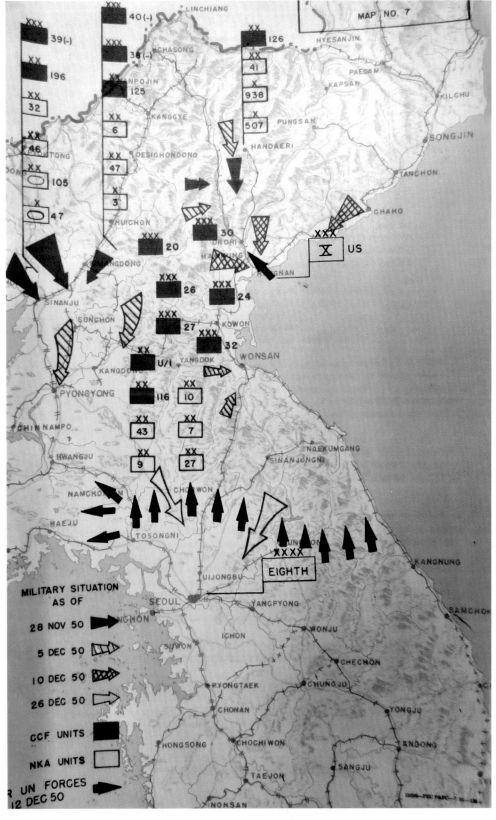

The military situation on the Korean Peninsula, December 1950. (Map United Nations)

The Statue of Brothers, Korean War Memorial, Seoul, depicting a South Korean soldier embracing one from North Korea in reconciliation. (Photo IMCOM)

Commandos of the British 41st Royal Marines, Sangjin. (Photo NARA)

Peng Dehuai's plan was materializing. In its war against Chinese Nationalist forces, the Communist Chinese had employed ambush tactics against more powerful foes that had been lured to advance into predetermined tactically advantageous sites. With nine armies now in North Korea, totalling more than 380,000 troops, Peng positioned the CPVA XIII Corps in the west and the CPVA VIII Corps in the east, to await the arrival of the advancing UN forces to spring his trap.

In the US Eighth Army sector, General Walker started to implement his assurances to MacArthur to recover lost ground during the Chinese first offensive. On 7 November, the 21st Regimental Combat Team, US 24th Division (US 21RCT), moved back across the Ch'ŏngch'ŏn River in divisional reserve.

In the 27th British Commonwealth Brigade (27th British) sector, Brigadier Basil Coad had the 3rd Battalion, Royal Australian Regiment (3RAR), spearhead the fresh advance to re-establish the river beachhead. The 1st Battalion, Argyll and Sutherland Highlanders (1/Argylls) moved next, followed by two companies of the 1st Battalion, Middlesex Regiment (1/Middlesex), reoccupying hill features to the south of Tang-dong and Pakch'ŏn. On the 1/Argylls' right flank, the 5th Regimental Combat Team, US 24th Division (US 5RCT) established contact with the Scottish battalion.

NOW THEY ARE THE COMPO AND PONCHO BRIGADE

From David Walker, with the British 29th Brigade in Korea, Sunday.
As from today it is Poncho and Compo for men of this brigade as they start to toughen up for a long winter. "Poncho" is a new style ground-sheet. When it is fixed to as entrenching tool two men can sleep beneath it. "Compo" means a change to British combat rations instead of the American food which the men have been enjoying up to now.

The "Poncho" decision was taken to accustom the men to Korean winter conditions; the "Compo" decision was made at high level in order to save dollars. "It's combat rations and no nonsense gets through after this," I was told yesterday as of the Ulsters ate dinner composed of cold spam, cooked frankfurters and no vegetables.

At brigade headquarters I saw a door marked "Snake Pit." Inside, men were having hot baths in drums that had once contained signals equipment.

It's Rugged Going
Mobile bakeries and bathing units are on the way, but for the time being the going is "rugged." Men have been issued this week-end with special string undervests. camouflaged windproof jackets and trousers to be worn over their battledress. and inner and outer gloves. And they are wearing Finnish ski-ing boots, which they broke in on board ship. Winter in this country will be the severest test of British ingenuity, but after seeing American troops in the front line I can state that the 29th Brigade will be the best equipped unit in Korea for arctic warfare.

Daily Mirror, 20 November 1950

By 10 November, the troops, including a reluctant ROKA 15th Regiment, had advanced to establish an incomplete line abreast of the Pakch'ŏn–Yŏngbyŏn axis. Brigadier Coad was forced to wait for the US 1st Cavalry Division's advance on Yŏngbyŏn. His advance had been unopposed, with his troops reporting evidence of a speedy enemy withdrawal, resulting in the brigadier coming to a premature conclusion in his war diary entry for 13 November: 'It is obvious that the enemy have broken contact and have withdrawn to the North. Their limited attempt to break through to the CHONGCHON River failed and it appears that they are not in a position and do not wish to resume the offensive.'*

On 17 November, Brigadier Coad received news that the US 1st Cavalry had secured Yŏngbyŏn. The 1/Middlesex, supported by Patton tanks of D Company, US 6th

* *27th British Commonwealth Brigade War Diary September to October 1950* (Australia War Memorial Archives, Campbell).

Tank Battalion, were tasked with patrolling Pakch'ŏn and establishing contact with ROKA 12th Regiment to their left, to ensure the line of communication southward toward the Ch'ŏngch'ŏn was kept clear. By this time, logistics had become a major problem. Constant sub-zero temperatures was causing vehicle engine blocks to crack, while critical shortages of fuel prevented the American armour from accompanying the 27th British patrols.

On 21 November, US I Corps commander, Major General Frank W. Milburn worked on the disposition of his troops along the front: the ROKA 11th Regiment (ROKA 11th) took over the US 5RCT positions and elements of the US 25th Division, commanded by Major General William B. Kean, relieved the US 19RCT. The US 24th Division, comprising the 5th, 19th and 25th RCTs now assembled a few miles south of Pakch'ŏn.

The following day, the 27th British was put into US I Corps reserve, while the US 24th Division and the ROKA 1st Division prepared to move north and north-west on the Yalu River, taking Chongju and Taech'ŏn as intermediate objectives.

The 27th British war diary entry for 25 November recorded: 'Today marked the opening day of the offensive which it is hoped would reach the Manchurian Border and finish the

Soldiers of the 3rd Battalion, Royal Australian Regiment, British 27th Brigade. (Photo Australian War Memorial)

It was very, very late when we got back to the company and found the kitchen there preparing Thanksgiving dinner. It was actually the day after Thanksgiving but no one minded.

We were served turkey and all the things that go with it on tin trays, just like aboard ships. Darker than pitch. We turned on the lights of jeeps and stood or sat on the hoods of the vehicles and ate our meal. I didn't give a good-sized damn because it was food and we hadn't had honest-to-God food in a long, long time.

You had to eat fast because everything was turning cold. The gravy then the mashed potatoes froze first. The inside of the turkey was still warm. Boy, you ate fast. And all the time the snipers were shooting at us.

Hospitalman Third Class William Davis, B Company, US 7th Marines[*]

[*] Donald Knox, *The Korean War, Pusan to Chosin: An Oral History* (Harcourt Brace & Co., Orlando, 1985).

Korean War."[*] Peng Dehuai's dupe to lure the unsuspecting UN forces into the trap set by his CPVA XIII Corps was working.

Throughout 26 November, as the US I Corps struck north, corps HQ received worrying signals of increased levels of contact with large numbers of enemy troops. The 21RCT had reached Chongju with little difficulty, but the US 19RCT reported a large concentration of the enemy in the hills north of Napch'ŏngjŏng. During the previous night, the ROKA 11th held their position under intense enemy fire. North of Yŏngbyŏn, the US 25th Division made contact with a substantial enemy force, while a company had been cut off on the division's left flank.

Shortly before midnight, Brigadier Coad was informed by US Eighth Army that his brigade was being transferred to US IX Corps command with immediate effect, and that he was expected to move first thing in the morning.

In the mountainous central plateau, flanked by US I Corps to the left and US X Corps the right, Major General John B. Coulter's US IX Corps was in a perilous situation with the collapse of the ROKA II Corps. The CPVA XXXVIII and XLII corps had inflicted major defeats on the ROKA 7th and 8th divisions, capturing Tŏkch'ŏn and moving on Kaech'ŏn. Large numbers of South Korean troops had been cut off, leaving the corps' left flank dangerously exposed. To the west of Yŏngdam-ni, the Chinese also attacked the left flank of the US 2nd Division, prompting General Walker to move the Turkish Brigade east along the Kaech'ŏn–Tŏkch'ŏn in an attempt to block the Chinese westward advance.

[*] *27th British Commonwealth Brigade War Diary September to October 1950* (Australia War Memorial Archives, Campbell).

1st Marine Tank Battalion armour in support of the Turkish Brigade. (Photo MSgt J.W. Hayes)

Commanded by General Tashin Yazici, the 5,000-strong Turkish unit had arrived in Pusan in mid-October and would now be facing their first action as they moved into position on the US 2nd Division's right flank.

Above Yŏngbyŏn, the US 25th Division was reported to be holding their position against the Chinese onslaught, while to the west the South Koreans were pushed back south-east of Taech'ŏn. The US 24th Division was pulled back to cover the rapidly deteriorating situation in the area.

On the night of 27 November, the 27th British was placed on an hour's notice to take up defensive positions toward Yongsan-dong. However, the provision at short notice of troop-lifting transport and marrying up with the intended support areas all but negated such a rapid move. That evening, there was open talk at US IX Corps HQ of a general withdrawal, in what history would call the Battle of Ch'ŏngch'ŏn as UN troops tried to hold a line along the river.

At Yongsan-dong to the west, the CPVA LXVI Corps attacked the ROKA 1st Infantry Division, US I Corps. In the centre, elements of the US IX Corps at Ipsŏk and Kujang-dong came under penetrating attacks from the CPVA XXXIX and XL corps. To the east, the CPVA XXXVIII and XLII corps breached the ROKA II Corps' line at Tŏkch'ŏn and Yongdŏk-ni.

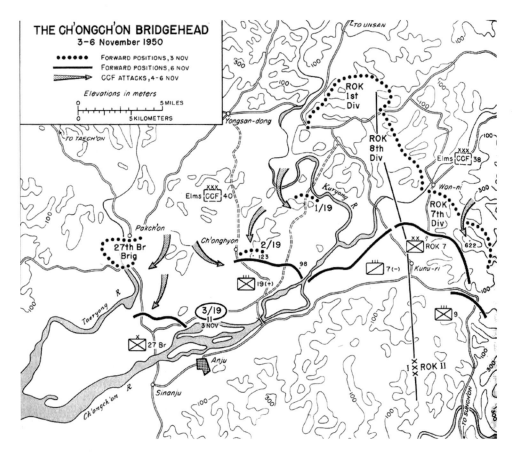

Ch'ŏngch'ŏn bridgehead, 3–6 November 1950.

The next day, US IX Corps described the situation as being critical. Communications with the defeated ROKA II Corps had been lost. With the collapse in the US Eighth Army's centre, the Chinese infiltrated the right of the US 2nd Division. With the US IX Corps in full retreat, Kunu-ri became a bottleneck. General Walker ordered the US 2nd Division to hold a new line at the town.

To the east of Kunu-ri, General Coulter ordered the Turkish Brigade from reserve to block the CPVA offensive from the east. However, in a series of battles over 28 and 29 November, the hapless Turks were overwhelmed by the 340th and 342nd regiments, CPVA 114th Division. Suffering casualties of 218 killed, 94 missing and 455 wounded, survivors that escaped the CPVA encirclement were attached to the US 2nd Division.

With the rapidly deteriorating situation in the US X Corps sector, General Walker's right flank was now weak and in imminent danger of collapsing. In Tokyo, having been briefed by the US Eighth Army commander, General MacArthur ordered the whole army to withdraw to a new line 30 miles south of Kunu-ri, or risk encirclement by the CPVA.

Walker's major units immediately broke off contact with the CPVA and withdrew, leaving the US 2nd Division as a rear guard.

However, as the division prepared to pull out, the US 38th Regiment (US 38th) came under attack from the CPVA 112th Division. While the GIs were able to withstand the Chinese assault and stand firm, on their right flank the much weaker Turkish Brigade was outflanked by the CPVA 114th Division. Attacking on the south bank of the Taedong River, the Chinese forces then crossed the river into Walker's rear areas. Facing certain envelopment, Turkish commander Brigadier Yazici withdrew, leaving the US 38th's right flank completely open.

At last light on 29 November, the Chinese cut the road between Kunu-ri and the US 38th, forcing the Americans to escape through the enemy's lines. At around 4 a.m. the next morning, the US 38th broke through and Kunu-ri fell to the Chinese.

Troop transport continued to plague the US IX Corps and many of the British and Australian troops had to march most of the way to the new area centred on Chasan. Just after 3 a.m. on the morning of 29 November, the last of the brigade battalions, 1/Middlesex, reported in. Later that day, an exhausted, frozen 1/Middlesex started patrolling the

American 8-inch howitzer. (Photo NARA)

north–south Sunchon–Kaech'ŏn road, but without armour or artillery support. The Australians were tasked with denying a CPVA crossing of the Taedong River from the east, while the 1/Argylls was held in brigade reserve.

As reports came in that the CPVA had cut the pass at Yongwŏn-ni in two-company strength, at the 27th British HQ the 1/Argylls received orders to move on the US

In his youth, he had been brought up on a diet of mass-produced Hollywood war movies, on books and poems and epics which glorified the deeds of war, brain-washed—like many of his generation—by the scriptwriters' propaganda and the skills of John Ford and Cecil B. de Mille and their like. Now Korea brought home the awful reality of the false impressions of war created to sell books and films. He learned, for example, that bullets fired in his direction did not seem at all like sounds created by Hollywood sound effects engineers, but sounded much more aggressive, like swarms of angry bees. That the bodies of the newly-dead were rubbery until stiffened by rigor mortis. Nothing like so much as the dead in John Wayne and Errol Flynn war movies.

Much of the survival experience for the frontline soldier depends upon a variety of purpose-built holes in the ground, and he learned to dig each one of them (hence the vulgar endearment "The Shitdiggers," which infantry soldiers call each other): hole to sleep in, holes to fight in, holes to hide away in, holes to escape in, holes to defecate in, holes for mortars and machine-guns, holes for mines and booby-traps and holes to bury your friends in! Each hole having its own authenticity of purpose and its own distinguishing name; no two being alike.

He learned, also, the skill in survival and living with other creatures trying to survive on him and others—rats, centipedes, snakes, leeches and creepy-crawlies of every kind as well as the ever present and persistent flies and mosquitoes. Learning the awful necessity of survival in the extremes of climate—the scorching heat of subtropical summers and the killer-cold of the sub-arctic winter—was an experience that would stay in his mind for ever, and nothing would cloud the images of recollection.

He learned to tolerate, albeit reluctantly, the perverse stench that offended the senses of everyone. This rose from the rice fields that were covered with human excreta, which had been ladled out of army field latrines by unfortunate young women, who were thus disfavoured with the stigma "shit-biddy," by the British Tommy.

National serviceman Gunner Denis Woods, Royal Artillery[*]

---

[*] Ashley Cunningham-Boothe and Peter Farrar, Eds., *British Forces in the Korean War* (British Korean Veterans Association, Halifax, 1997).

5th Cavalry Regiment's (US 5th Cav) left flank. From here, the battalion would patrol forward to Chusong-dong.

Arriving at Yongwŏn-ni at around midday, 1/Middlesex took the foothills about 1,000 yards from the higher hills flanking the pass. Upon being mortared by the Chinese, A Company launched an attack on the west side of the pass, but were met with heavy small-arms and machine-gun fire. A second company joined the attack, but without tank and artillery support, the British troops were forced to call off the attack, and eventually withdrew at 4 p.m. to nearby Choptong. The battalion suffered twenty-six casualties, including one killed.

At 3 a.m. on 30 November, US IX Corps ordered the 27th British to hold the area immediately to the south of the Chinese-held Yongwŏn-ni Pass to provide maximum support to the US 2nd Division which was planning to break through from the north. At 10.30, 1/Middlesex was in position, with an artillery battery and tanks in support. While engaging a CPVA presence south of the pass, five American tanks and soft-skin vehicles of the US 2nd Division appeared from the pass, having run a gauntlet of heavy enemy fire.

Troops on foot followed, many of them wounded. Before long, 1/Middlesex Tac HQ was swamped with American casualties waiting to be processed and evacuated to a clearing station at Choptong. In the disjointed throng, any semblance of leadership evaporated, with some of the GIs, not believing that they were safe, continued to discharge their rifles, causing casualties among the Middlesex troops in attendance. By 3 p.m., the seemingly endless flow of stragglers finally ceased, and 1/Middlesex was authorized to withdraw to the brigade area, doing so under enemy fire from the hills on both flanks.

A massive influx of refugees heading south now compounded the rapidly worsening position an already overtaxed Brigadier Coad was facing. To stop the refugees, 3RAR was

M46 tanks of the US Army 6th Tank Battalion, painted with tiger stripes and faces. (Photo NARA)

ordered to block the two fords through the Taedong River and 1/Argylls to impose a curfew on the two villages on the main road to Sunchon.

With the arrival in Korea of the British 29th, came desperately needed winter kit for the British 27th. The upper reaches of the Yalu had frozen over in places, while MacArthur's forces struggled with the bitterly cold conditions. British tanks were being parked on straw so that the tracks would not freeze onto the ground, the tank crews starting the tanks every half hour to keep them serviceable.

Private First Class (PFC) Fred Davison of the US 5th Marines, speaking of his own miserable situation, accurately summed up how most of the UN troops felt in late November, facing a powerful new foe in sub-zero North Korea:

> We had "warming tents" set up on the reverse slope of every hill we occupied for the night. There were so many of us and so few tents that it became impossible to stay in the tents long enough to even approach getting warm. It was always time to leave and go back on the line so someone else could use the tents. The days and nights rolled into a blend of light and dark. There was always a hill to climb and it was always cold! When it snowed it was cold. When the sun shone it was cold. When we marched north it was cold. When we marched south it was cold. And I was tired. I'd been in combat since August 2 in the Pusan Perimeter; I'd been twice on the slopes of Obongni Ridge; I'd landed at Inch'on; I'd crossed the Han and fought in Seoul. I was tired and damned near ready to give up the ghost.[*]

The 27th British war diary records fresh orders had been received from HQ US 1st Cavalry Division for Brigadier Coad's unit. In a 'strange' move, the brigade was ordered to turn around and relieve the US 5th Cavalry who were holding blocking positions north of Sunchon. General Gay planned to shorten the line south of Sunchon so that the town could be held until large quantities of ammunition were trucked south'.[†]

Having routed the ROKA 6th Infantry Division, the CPVA XLII Corps continued to advance southward, resulting in General Gay withdrawing the US 7th Cavalry. A fierce battle soon raged between the Americans and the CPVA 125th Division, while the CPVA XXXVIII Corps made an unhindered move on the Kunu-ri–Sunchon road.

Temporarily coming under the command of the US 7th Cavalry, which also included a battalion of the US 8th Cavalry that had suffered major losses at Unsan, Brigadier Coad would bolster the defence bridgehead south-east of Sunchon.

---

[*] Donald Knox, *The Korean War, Pusan to Chosin: An Oral History* (Harcourt Brace & Co., Orlando, 1985).

[†] *27th British Commonwealth Brigade War Diary September to October 1950* (Australia War Memorial Archives, Campbell).

Early on the morning of 30 November, Major General Laurence B. Keiser, commanding US 2nd Division, ordered his troops to withdraw along the main road to Sunchon. But by this time, the CPVA 112th and 113th divisions occupied the valley through which the road from Kunu-ri passed, creating a roadblock 6 miles in depth. Leading the US 2nd Division, Colonel Charles C. Sloane's US 9th Regiment soon ran into heavy machine-gun and mortar fire, stalling the division's withdrawal.

Assessing the situation, and based on the belief that the Chinese roadblock was not very deep and with the 1/Middlesex to the south of the enemy position, at 10 a.m., Keiser ordered the division to break through the blockade. The outcome—running 'the Gauntlet'—was a disaster for the US 2nd Division.

The Chinese let loose with everything they had, the Americans' passage littered with damaged and destroyed transport and dead and wounded troops. Such was the desperate rush to get through the kill zone, the wounded were left where they fell in roadside ditches. Overhead, air support met with limited success, returning to base as darkness descended. Having become masters at night combat, the CPVA destroyed the US 38th and the US 503rd Artillery Battalion, effectively resealing the roadblock. To the US 2nd Division's rear, Colonel Paul L. Freeman elected to divert his US 23rd Regiment (US 23rd) west along the Anju road to circumvent the Chinese barrier to their retreat. The decision was also made to fire off its remaining stock of artillery and tank shells. In twenty-two minutes, a barrage of more than 3,200 shells forced the CPVA to break off its pursuit of the US 23rd.

In the valley, the beaten US 2nd Division abandoned all their vehicles to start the long walk through the hills and, hopefully, safety. On 1 December, the last of the division's troops, lacking any semblance of unit cohesion, staggered into Sunchon. The following day, the US Eighth Army lost all contact with the Chinese forces.

The US 2nd Division Korean war diary provides the epilogue for one of the darkest weeks in the division's history:

> As the period came to a close, the battered 2d Infantry Division was assembling at Chasan and plans were being made for another move to Chunghwa where it was to go into Eighth Army reserve. Straggler collecting points were set up in Sunchon and teams were sent north as far as possible to pick up wounded stragglers.
>
> Losses in personnel and equipment had been very severe. The casualties for the month totalled over 5,000 men, of which approximately 90% occurred during the period from 25–30 November. Losses in equipment were also extremely heavy. The 2d Division had met the full impact of an overwhelming Chinese force, had slowed an attack which might have destroyed the Eighth Army, and withdrew with its basic organization intact. It now needed a period of rest to regroup and resupply, and to rest the men who had served so valiantly.[*]

---

[*] Korean War Project: www.koreanwar.org/

General Walker's advance on the Yalu lasted a day, as eighteen divisions of the CPVA 13th Army Group brought the US Eighth Army to an abrupt halt that rapidly turned into a rout. From late on 29 November to the night of 30 November, the US 2nd Division sustained 3,000 men killed, missing and wounded. Almost all of its equipment and ordnance lay abandoned along the Kunu-ri–Sunchon road. It would take six months to reconstitute the division to combat capabilities. The virtual annihilation of the three divisions of the ROKA II Corps by five Chinese divisions was an even greater disaster.

Between 25 November and 2 December 1950, the US Eighth Army suffered 11,000 casualties.

5. A PLACE CALLED CHOSIN

The Eagle does not catch flies!
But, have you seen the flies when the Eagle dies?
Flyblown Fusiliers that the maggots eat;
No cool graveyard for them in their defeat.

One Time Out of History's Calendar'
Ashley Cunningham-Boothe
Royal Northumberland Fusiliers[*]

In mid-morning 21 November, three battalions of 17RCT, US 7th Infantry Division, won General MacArthur's race for the Yalu River on the border with Chinese Manchuria. Walking unopposed into Hyesanjin on the south bank, the Americans found the whole hutted North Korean village in ruins after an earlier attack by carrier-borne US Navy aircraft. At this point the Yalu was only 50 to 75 feet wide and almost frozen over.

Like other American units in North Korea, the US 7th Division was ill-prepared for the life-threatening sub-zero winter conditions. An attempt at a river crossing—the bridge had been destroyed—was aborted due to the freezing water. Eighteen members of the patrol sustained frostbite and had to have their uniforms cut off. Blood plasma could not be administered before being warmed up for ninety minutes and water-based medication froze.

For the command staff, however, the achievement of the cold and tired soldiers was a triumph, warranting a photo call in which General Almond, commanding the US X Corps, Major General David Barr, the US 7th Infantry Division, and Colonel Herbert Powell, commanding officer of the US 17th RCT, were snapped as they smilingly looked across the Yalu. After reading a congratulatory signal from General MacArthur in Tokyo, General Almond, in conveying the supremo's gratitude to General Barr, said:

> The fact that only twenty days ago this division landed amphibiously over the beaches at Iwon and advanced 200 miles over tortuous mountain terrain and fought successfully against a determined foe in subzero weather will be regarded in history as an outstanding military achievement.[†]

As the other US 7th Division units neared their own objectives on the Yalu, around 100 miles to the south-west, the US 1st Marine Division was inching its way along the main

---

[*] Ashley Cunningham-Boothe and Peter Farrar, Eds., *British Forces in the Korean War* (British Korean Veterans Association, Halifax, 1997).

[†] James McGovern, *To the Yalu: From the Chinese Invasion of Korea to MacArthur's Dismissal* (William Morrow, New York, 1972).

Frostbite casualties of the embattled US 1st Marine Division and US 7th Infantry Division await medical evacuation. (Photo NARA)

supply route toward the Changjin Reservoir, the North Korean name for the Japanese-occupation name, Chosin. The division's slow progress was deliberate as its commander, Major General Oliver P. Smith, did not share the prevalent euphoria of victory at the sudden withdrawal of the invading Chinese armies. He did not believe that they would be home for Christmas. In a letter to the commandant of the US Marine Corps, General Clifton B. Cates, Smith did not hold back:

> Someone in high authority will have to make up his mind as to what is our goal. My mission is still to advance to the border. The Eighth Army, 80 miles to the southwest, will not attack until the 20th [November]. Manifestly, we should not push on without regard to the Eighth Army. We would simply get further out on a limb.
>
> If the Eighth Army push does not go, then the decision will have to be made as to what to do next. I believe a winter campaign in the mountains of North Korea is too much to ask of the American soldier or marine, and I doubt the feasibility of supplying troops in this area during the winter or providing for the evacuation of sick and wounded.*

The ever-pragmatic General Smith was not prepared to place his men at risk by stringing his division out for than 120 miles along a narrow mountain track: the distance in air

---

* Ibid.

Corpsmen of the US 1st Marine Division in the frozen Changjin terrain. (Photo USMC)

miles from the port city of Hamhung to his divisional command post. Smith would not allow himself to be cajoled into increasing his pace beyond a mile a day. Upon reaching Yudam-ni on the south-western shores of Changjin Reservoir, the general meticulously consolidated and strengthened his situation in what he firmly believed to be dangerously hostile.

The dispositions of his three regiments came first. At Yudam-ni itself, the 7th Regiment (US 7th Marines), under Colonel Homer L. Litzenberg, would establish a blocking position. At Hagaru-ri, 15 miles to the south-east, Lieutenant Colonel Raymond L. Murray's 5th Regiment (US 5th Marines) would take up a position protecting the division's rear. The 1st Regiment (US 1st Marines), commanded by Colonel Lewis B. 'Chesty' Puller, remained well back on the main supply route to Hŭngnam.

General Smith's next priority was the construction of an airstrip to facilitate medical evacuation and the inflow of ammunition and supplies. Stocks were also transferred to Hagaru-ri. The road to the coast also received attention, to accommodate tanks and trucks, and as an improved route of retreat if the need arose.

Hŭngnam became the main referral hospital for casualties, with the divisional hospital capacity being increased to 400 beds. Having arrived in Korea from Norfolk on 16 August, the Haven-class hospital ship, USS *Consolation* (AH-15), sailed for Hŭngnam, bringing with her an extra 802 beds and more than 500 medical personnel. Hagaru-ri would become a forward surgical unit into which medical staff would be flown from Hŭngnam, while clearing stations were set up along the main supply route.

The US Eighth Army was scheduled to jump off on 24 November to continue the UN's advance. Three days later, the Marines were assigned to strike west to close the gap with General Walker's troops, in what General MacArthur termed a 'giant U.N. pincer'.

On 25 November, General Smith received Corps Operation Order 7, directing his division to go on the offensive at 8 a.m. on 27 November. His objective would be to sever

CRISIS IN KOREA

The most urgent and immediate task in Korea is a military one. It is for the United Nations forces to halt the new Chinese attack and to establish a line they can hold. General MacArthur's all-over-by-Christmas offensive has failed. Some observers were surprised it ever started. At least it has established the fact of Chinese intervention in strength under the authority of the Peking Government. Few people in the West could have believed the previous story of intervention by volunteers only. It is now exposed as a complete fabrication. General MacArthur estimates that 200,000 regular Chinese troops are in North Korea. Military intelligence has proved a rather deceptive guide so far in Korea. But there can be no doubt of the critical position in which United Nations forces are now placed, or that Chinese troops—operating with supplies and reserves in the sanctuary of Manchuria—have had an unexpected success. How far China is prepared to exploit the situation is not known. Obviously, General MacArthur must hit back as hard as he can, and be given every assistance to do so. No one is needed to instruct him on how to carry out his military duty. But, as he says in his historic communiqué, the new situation poses issues beyond the authority of the military command—issues which must find their solution in the councils of the United Nations.

At the Security Council, yesterday, a quick beginning was made in taking up the issues. The United States delegate accused Communist China of open aggression in Korea. The representative of Peking did not answer his charges, but, instead, accused America of violating the Manchurian border. China must learn that it is not America alone, but the United Nations, she is accusing. If she still thinks the United Nations in Korea intend to violate Manchurian territory, no effort should be spared to convince her that this is not so. Her own present aggressive action is the worst way of preserving her territory.

Editorial, *Liverpool Echo*, 29 November 1950

Medical transfer from a Mobile Army Surgical Hospital (MASH). (Photo US Army)

enemy lines of communication at Mup'yŏng-ni to the north-west, before advancing on the Yalu River, clearing a zone to the Manchurian border of all enemy forces.

Meanwhile, the US 5th Marines held positions to the east of Changjin, waiting to move west when relieved by elements of the US 7th Marines. While the US 1st Marines remained in reserve, at 8 a.m. on 27 November, the US 5th Marines passed through the US 7th Marines west of Yudam-ni. At this time, the reinforced British 41st (Independent) Commando, Royal Marines, attached to the American marine division, prepared to move to Yudam-ni once the village was taken.

The 3rd Battalion, US 7th Marines (US 3/7th Marines) achieved this objective on the afternoon of 25 November, finding the village abandoned except for scattered bodies of Chinese soldiers from earlier airstrikes. Aerial reconnaissance, however, revealed that the enemy were now dug in, with artillery, only a short distance away, to which is was concluded that: 'the lack of aggressiveness thus far characteristic of enemy forces known to be located in the area, are factors indicative of his general defensive attitude. The threat to the Division flank and MSR was reiterated'.*

---

* *1st Marine Division Historical Diary – November 1950* (National Archives and Records Administration, College Park Maryland).

To the east of the US X Corps sector, Major General David G. Barr's US 7th Infantry Division had moved from south of Hyesanjin to assume a new zone of action in the Changjin Reservoir area. The US 17th Regiment (US 17/7th), commanded by Colonel Herbert B. Powell, attacked along the Kapsan–P'ungsan axis, while the US 31st Regiment (US 31/7th), under Colonel Allan D. MacLean, was held in reserve, responsible for keeping the main supply route clear. The US 32nd Regiment (US 32/7th), commanded by Colonel Charles M. Mount, patrolled and executed reconnaissance missions from the northern reaches of the Changjin Reservoir to the Yalu.

During the two days of 24 and 25 November, patrols from the US 17/7th and US 31/7th came under constant enemy fire as the Chinese tested the UN forces' positions and strengths. On 26 November, Lieutenant Colonel Don Faith's 1,053-strong 1st Battalion, US 32/7th, arrived at the south-eastern tip of the reservoir to relieve Marine units. Information gleaned from Chinese POWs revealed that the 58th, 59th and 60th divisions of the CPVA XX Corps had moved into the area with orders to cut the UN forces' main supply route. Still under orders to continue the advance on the Yalu, Colonel Faith harboured the next two nights at his position on the reservoir, arranging his troops in all-round defence perimeters.

On the move at Changjin. (Photo NARA)

At 10 p.m. on the night of 27 November, Faith met with his company commanders at the battalion command post to issue attack orders for the following morning. Shortly after midnight, officer commanding A Company, Captain Edward B. Scullion, and executive officer First Lieutenant Cecil G. Smith, responded to firing from the three platoons on the company's right flank. Visibility in the darkness was poor resulting in an inconclusive outcome.

About half an hour later, the Chinese, estimated at company strength, hit both flanks of the three platoons, surrounding the command post and penetrating the 60mm mortar position. Dashing forward to the left flank of Third Platoon, Captain Scullion was shot and killed. Captain Robert F. Haynes assumed command of A Company, but he too was killed in the fighting. Lieutenant Smith now took command, forming a perimeter around the command post until first light when the Chinese broke off their attack.

On General Barr's left flank, the US 7th Marines had arrived at Yudam-ni, where commanding officer, Colonel Homer L. Litzenberg, was ordered to re-orientate his northward advance to link up with the US Eighth Army's left flank 70 miles across mountainous terrain. Once in place, General MacArthur envisaged an enormous pincer movement that would trap the enemy against the Yalu and bring the war to an end. The US 5th Marines, commanded by Lieutenant Colonel Raymond L. Murray, once relieved by the 1st Battalion, US 32/7th Division east of the Changjin Reservoir, would pass through the US 7th Marines to spearhead the Marines' westward advance on General Walker's right flank at Mup'yŏng-ni. Within hours, however, Mao's peasant hordes in uniform left MacArthur's grand strategy in tatters.

That same day, the 2nd Battalion, US 1st Marine Regiment (US 2/1st Marines), under Lieutenant Colonel Allan Sutter, arrived at Koto-ri to relieve the 2nd Battalion, US 5th Marine Regiment (US 2/5th Marines), and establish regimental headquarters. From here, the US 5th Marines, moved north, first to Hagaru-ri, then north-east through the Tŏkdong Pass to Yudam-ni to the east of the Changjin Reservoir. Leaving G Company in reserve at Koto-ri, H and I companies, 3rd Battalion, US 1st Marine Regiment (US 3/1st Marines), reached Hagaru-ri at last light.

On the main supply route to the south, at Chinhŭng-ni the 1st Battalion, US 1st Marine Regiment (US 1/1st Marines) guarded the southern entrance to the strategic Funchilin Pass. Commanded by Lieutenant Colonel Donald M. Schmuck, the battalion came under only light probing attacks from elements of the CPVA.

Sat on the southern reaches of the Changjin Reservoir, the hamlet of Hagaru-ri was of major tactical importance to General Smith as the site of his divisional HQ and an airfield. Concurrent commander of the US 3/1st Marines and the Hagaru-ri Defence Force, Lieutenant Colonel Thomas L. Ridge was fully aware that his defence line was extremely thin. After touring the 4-mile perimeter with battalion S3 (operations), Major Joseph Trumpeter and Weapons Company commander, Major Edward Simmons, Ridge reached the disturbing conclusion that his task required two regiments, and not the two rifle companies at his disposal.

Marine with an image of Joseph Stalin found in a bunker, Yudam-ni, 27 November 1950. (Photo USMC)

At the north-eastern corner of his perimeter, Ridge positioned the 105mm howitzers of H Battery, US 11th Marines. Having recently arrived with the US 3/1st Marines, D Battery was positioned to the south-east. Using men from elements of the Weapons Company, the Service Battalion and the divisional HQ battalion, Ridge formed defence units for the rest of his perimeter.

At Yudam-ni, early on 27 November, the US 5th Marines was preparing to pass through the US 7th Marines, with the objective of severing the Chinese line of communication at Mup'yŏng-ni to the north-west. The village of Yudam-ni was situated in a wide valley, large swathes of it covered by the Changjin Reservoir. The US 7th Marines commanded four of the five ridges surrounding the village, the fifth being the Northwest Ridge.

Two days earlier, Lieutenant Colonel Don Faith's US 1/32nd had arrived at the reservoir near Sinhung-ni to replace the US 5th Marines. Commander Colonel Murray advised Faith, now attached to the US 31st Infantry Regiment (31RCT) to establish a battalion command post against Hill 1221, near the village of Twiggae. He was instructed not to move north unless ordered to do so. However, based on intelligence that the area was 'safe', Colonel Faith instead sought and received authority from the US 31st commanding officer, Colonel Allan D. MacLean, to move north to Hudong-ni where he established his command post in a school building.

At 10 p.m. on 26 November, at US 5th Marines HQ, Colonel Murray met with his staff and officers to finalize plans for the advance due to jump off at 8 a.m. the next morning. The US 2/5th Marines would spearhead the attack, with close air support for the day by Vought F4U Corsair fighters from VMF-312 ('Checkerboards') stationed at Wŏnsan. The US 7th Marines were to support the attack by striking to the south-west. Thirty 105mm howitzers from the US 11th Marines would support the troops from positions at Yudam-ni,

Lieutenant Colonel Don Faith. (Photo NARA)

together with a lone M26 Pershing tank, the only armour available to Murray. The first objective in the advance to the Yalu was to be Yongnim-dong, 27 miles to the west.

At the same time, Colonel Litzenberg briefed his US 7th Marine officers. An infantry company would patrol southward in the direction of Hagaru-ri to ensure that the road remained secure. The US 3/7th Marines was to extend its disposition on Northwest Ridge, while H Company would dig in on Hill 403 commanding the road to the west.

At 5 a.m., 27 November, the Marine howitzers shelled the hills on either side of the road emerging from Yudam-ni. Jumping off at 8 a.m., F Company, US 2/5th Marines, came under small-arms fire as they set off for the gap between hills 1403 and 1426. Stalled, the Americans could only continue after six Corsairs had pounded the enemy positions. Joined by D Company, F Company had only advanced one mile by mid-afternoon, when they were ordered to establish a defensive position. As the enemy contact intensified, the US 3/7th Marines' progress was as slow, and they too were instructed to harbour for the night where they were.

Throughout the night of 27/28 November, the two US Marine regiments came under heavy attack from elements of the CPVA. In the morning, the realization had to be accepted that the Chinese had cut the main supply route between Yudam-ni and Hagaru-ri, and between Hagaru-ri and Koto-ri. Heavy enemy fire on both sections of the road forced convoys to abandon attempts to get through. General Smith ordered his two regiments at Yudam-ni to hold their advance pending clarification of the situation. Several attempts made by a battalion of the US 7th Marines to re-establish the main supply route to Hagaru-ri failed.

Marines between Yudam-ni and Hagaru-ri. (Photo USMC)

General Smith now surmised that the Chinese intended taking Hagaru-ri, held only by the US 3/1st Marines, less one company, divisional headquarters staff and service personnel. As a consequence, Smith ordered Task Force Drysdale to immediately move from Koto-ri to Hagaru-ri. Commanded by Lieutenant-Colonel Douglas Drysdale, the unit comprised the 41 (Independent) Commando, Royal Marines—attached to the US 1st Marine Division—B Company, US 1/31st; D Company, 1st Tank Battalion, USMC; G Company, 1st Marines; and headquarters troops. A Second World War commando veteran, Drysdale was chief instructor at the Royal Marines officer school.

In the mountains of the quadrant north-west of Yudam-ni, the US 5th and 7th Marines faced the massed forces of the CPVA XX Corps, under the leadership of Zhang Yixiang. Positioned from north to south, the corps comprised four divisions: the CPVA 89th Division (Yu Guangmao), the CPVA 59th Division (Dai Kelen), the CPVA 58th Division (Huang Chaotian) and the CPVA 60th Division (Chen Ting). To the east, two divisions—76th and 77th—of the CPVA XXVI Corps had jumped off eastward to cut the main supply route between Koto-ri and Hagaru-ri. And north of the Changjin Reservoir, the 79th and 80th divisions, CPVA XXVII Corps, executed a two-prong southerly attack on Yudam-ni and Hundong-ni.

To the east of the reservoir, Major General David Goodwin Bar's US 7th Infantry Division, having only just replaced the US Marine units at Hundong-ni, now came under

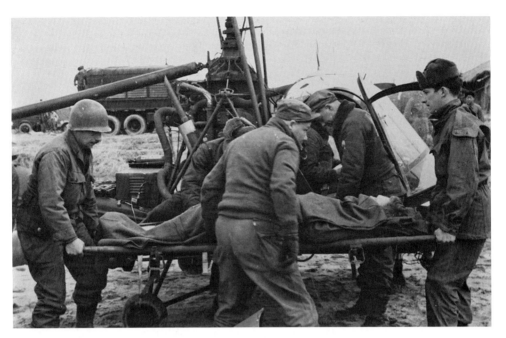

Helicopter evacuation of a wounded American from a forward clearing station. (Photo NARA)

heavy small-arms and automatic Chinese fire on the night of 28 November. Both B and A companies, US 1/32nd, were overrun, but the assailants were successfully driven off. By 8 p.m., the battalion aid station had handled 100 casualties. The following night, in another attack the CPVA pushed back A Company's flank while penetrating B Company defences. Counterattacks again restored the battalion lines.

With ammunition running low, at 4.30 a.m. on 29 November, the US 1/32nd attacked south along the road to link up with the US 3/31st. Encountering a roadblock, the battalion halted while two companies traversed adjacent hills to knock out the enemy roadblock. At the time, enemy fire appeared to come from the direction of the US 3/31st position, prompting Colonel MacLean to attempt a crossing of an inlet of the reservoir in that direction to stop what he took to be friendly fire. As he crossed, he was hit several times by small-arms fire, but managed to reach the opposite shore. A subsequent search of the area failed to find any trace of him. MacLean was listed as missing in action, before being presumed dead in March 1954. At 12.30 p.m., the US 1/32nd closed with the US 3/31st.

The latter had been under attack from around 1 a.m. on 28 November, with K Company and elements of I Company taking the brunt of the Chinese assault on their positions. The CPVA soldiers came so close that the American infantrymen were caught in artillery crossfire of the Chinese and the US 57th Field Artillery Battalion (FAB). Forced to withdraw, K Company pulled back to high ground into A Battery, US 57th FAB positions. Three hours later, the Chinese penetrated the A Battery perimeter, causing the gunners and K Company to fall back on B Battery where I Company had its tactical command post.

At first light the Chinese broke off their attack, but a mile to the south, D Battery, US 15th Anti-aircraft Artillery (US 15th AAA), and headquarters US 57th FAB came under enemy mortar fire. The CPVA attacked the position, but were fought off. Adjacent A Battery, US 57th FAB successfully held their position by point-blank fire at the charging CPVA.

Daylight hours were spent in an urgent consolidation and bolstering of a defensive position. Lieutenant Colonel William Reidy, commander of the US 3/31st, drew the perimeter tighter and withdrew troops from higher ground to strengthen his defences. The US 57th FAB batteries and the anti-aircraft battery were brought into the perimeter, while .50-calibre and 40mm-calibre heavy machine guns were placed at key positions.

At around 6 p.m. the Chinese attacked, but K and L companies—merged because of heavy losses—with the artillery and heavy-calibre machine guns repelled night-long attacks by the enemy. Typically, with daylight —29 November—the Chinese broke off the attack, leaving the Americans' stocks of ammunition dangerously depleted, with forty 105mm shells and no 40mm rounds left.

During the day the US 1/32nd linked up from the north and a consolidated task force formed with Colonel Faith in command of the combined US 1/32nd, US 3/31st and the US 57th FAB.

Marines launch a 4.5-inch rocket barrage against the Chinese. (Photo USMC)

Meanwhile at Hundong-ni, the previous day a force comprising the US 31st Tank Company (Sherman M4A3E8 tanks) and a composite infantry platoon drawn from C Company, US 13th Engineers Battalion, US 31st Anti-tank Mine platoon and headquarters personnel, jumped off to clear the road north in the direction of Colonel Faith's forces. General Henry I. 'Hammering Hank' Hodes, assistant commanding general, US 7th Infantry Division, accompanied the tanks. Approaching the site where the US 31st Medical Company had been ambushed during the night, the tank column came under CPVA attack from surrounding high ground that American infantry had not been able to secure. Taking fire from enemy anti-tank guns and 3.5-inch rocket launchers, the force sustained many casualties and lost four tanks before withdrawing.

General Hodes dispatched an urgent signal to General Barr requesting an extra battalion, but the US 2/31st was held up at Koto-ri. At 8 a.m. the following morning—29 November—another attempt was made to break through the Chinese line, but this too ended in failure. An hour later, a platoon of tanks undertook a reconnaissance mission to find an alternative route northward. None was found, but the tanks were attacked, during which two officers were killed and two tanks lost. At 3.30 p.m. the US 2/31st received orders to set off immediately for General Hodes's position. The Chinese continued to build up their presence.

That same morning, B Company, US 31st, joined Task Force Drysdale under command of the British 41 (Independent) Commando, attached US 1st Marine Regiment. With the objective of re-joining its parent unit, B Company had been tasked to assist Colonel Drysdale to clear the main supply route to Hagaru-ri. However, the trucks required to transport the company had not arrived and the task force set off without them.

More than four hours later, B Company was loaded and, without the support of armour, followed Drysdale's force. At around 6 p.m., the company came under enemy automatic fire, hand grenade and mortar attack. The Marine tanks tailing the column turned around when the firing started to protect the trucks behind them. Shortly before dawn the next morning—30 November—firing ceased and a CPVA commander demanded the Americans lay down their arms. Major Suley, senior Marine officer, refused, electing instead to fight his way back to Koto-ri, sustaining heavy losses as he went.

To the south, a lack of US X Corps transport delayed the US 2/31st at Majŏn-dong for nearly two days. It transpired that the trucks, carrying ammunition, had passed through on the morning of 29 November. The convoy had failed to stop to unload the ammunition and to pick up the waiting infantry battalion. At first light on 30 November, the battalion was finally trucked north, meeting light resistance as they went. At 1 a.m. the following morning, the column came under heavy attack two miles south of Koto-ri. F, G and elements of H companies fought their way forward, arriving at Koto-ri nearly two hours later. However, it would be mid-morning before the rest of the battalion staggered into the town.

Through 28 and 29 November, the US 1st Marine Regiment battalions held their respective defensive positions along the main supply route: the US 3/1st Marines at Hagaru-ri, the 2/1st Marines at Koto-ri and the 1/1st Marines farthest south at Chinhŭng-ni.

Between Hagaru-ri and Koto-ri, troops pass wreckage resulting from the ambush of the Task Force Drysdale column on 29 November. (Photo USMC)

Fourteen mountainous miles above Hagaru-ri, the US 5th and 7th Marine regiments held Yudam-ni. Ten understrength companies occupied the hills overlooking the village, while two battalions of the US 5th Marines had dug in on the valley floor. Four miles away at the base of the Tŏkdong Pass, C Company, US 7th Marines had taken up a position. At the top of the pass, F Company, US 7th Marines, held an isolated outpost.

As the moon rose over 'Fox Hill', F Company commander, Captain Barber, checked on his defences for the night. Sound-powered phones connected the company command post with mortars. Barber ordered a watch on the phone, comprising one officer and one NCO at all times during the hours of darkness.

At 4 a.m., Barber was woken to be informed that there were people approaching on the road. Moments later, F Company came under heavy fire from the north, west and south of the Marine perimeter. The mortars and Second and Third platoons were hit simultaneously. PFC Ernest Gonzalez relates:

> I saw a squad of Chinese moving to my left. I aimed, the light of the moon reflected
> off the rifle barrel, and fired. A man went down. Every time I spotted a grenade

Tanks on the perimeter of Koto-ri. (Photo USMC)

I yelled a warning and ducked. Some exploded, some didn't. In front, I saw the flick-ering light of a Chinese automatic weapon firing in my direction. I could not get a shot at it and had no grenades. I saw a second Chinese squad to my right rear. I fired and another man went down. The Marines in my foxhole warned me not to fire as it drew fire from the enemy. I thought, What the hell are we here for but to fire on the enemy when we see him?

The BAR [Browning automatic rifle] man was wounded by a grenade but continued to fire. More Marines joined us. There was an explosion. I turned and saw a Marine behind me bleeding from his forehead and mouth. He had shielded me from the blast. My fire-team leader was in a foxhole on my left with a machine gun. Throughout the night I saw the Chinese trying to reach him with grenades. Finally, some of them were able to get into his foxhole. The Chinese left him for dead and made off with the machine gun. A grenade went off in the connecting trench. I saw the flash and felt the shock wave. Several Marines were wounded by it. I was protected by the curve of the foxhole. Of the six Marines with me, I was now the only one not wounded. Whenever I killed a Chinese, I wanted to cheer, but realized if I did so, I might get careless. I had butterflies in my stomach and my shivering was not caused by the cold.[*]

---

[*] Donald Knox, *The Korean War, Pusan to Chosin: An Oral History* (Harcourt Brace & Co., Orlando, 1985)

Lieutenant Robert McCarthy's Third Platoon was hardest hit, the front two squads and machine-gun section completely overwhelmed by imponderable numbers of screaming Chinese soldiers. Of the thirty-five Marines in these units, fifteen were killed, nine wounded and three missing—only eight remained combat effective.

The CPVA now directed their attention on the 1st Squad's left and centre fire teams. The hilltop lit up with the almost continuous exploding American and Chinese grenades. PFC Harrison Pommers had three grenades go off in his foxhole and a fourth explode on his helmet, knocking him out. When he came to, he started directing his fire team once more.

On the platoon's left, Private Smith's fire team was on the verge of collapsing when their leader and the Browning automatic rifle (BAR) man were killed. Seeing the danger, Private Hector Cafferata and another Marine from Second Platoon stepped in, preventing the CPVA from breaking through Third Platoon's left.

In stockinged feet, as he had had no time to put on his boots, Cafferata stood up and, under heavy fire, fired two M1 rifles as fast as a wounded Marine next to him was able to reload. He also threw a CPVA grenade out of their trench and knocked away two more from the parapet. His gallantry would earn him the Medal of Honor.

In the melee of close-quarter combat as the Marines of F Company frantically fought for their lives on Fox Hill, First Lieutenant Lawrence Schmitt discovered that their mortars had been abandoned. Five members of the 81mm mortar team, including the section leader, were sheltering behind a disused hut. Schmitt dashed across open ground to the hut to rally the men to recover the two vital support weapons. Together with another three Marines who had joined the team behind the hut, Schmitt led the men on a sprint to the mortars in a clearing near the command post. With individuals responsible for a baseplate or a tube or a bipod, the recovery was successful and without any casualties. The equipment was lugged back up the slope from where the reconstituted teams quickly commenced registering fire on CPVA positions.

The corpsmen on Fox Hill miraculously survived the night, but with severe casualties and low stocks of ammunition. In the dark, Gunnery Sergeant Bunch directed a team of Marines administering medical assistance to fifty-four wounded troops. By candlelight, in a makeshift aid station at an abandoned hut, wounds were dressed as best possible and efforts made to keep the casualties warm. Morphine syrettes were warmed up in their mouths before being injected. Tragically, the plasma was frozen and, with no means to thaw the bottled contents, Marines were dying for the lack of it.

At 10.30 a.m., the airstrike requested by Captain Barber on a ridge to the north-west of Fox Hill took place. Eight P-51 Mustangs of No. 77 Squadron, Royal Australian Air Force (RAAF), bombed and rocketed the Chinese positions and strafed the valley on either side of the Yudam-ni road. Initially based at Iwakuni, the Australian squadron became the first non-American UN unit to enter the war when it flew sorties on 2 July 1950.

During the day cargo aircraft dropped ammunition and essential medical supplies to Barber. At Yudam-ni, Colonel Litzenberg, commanding the US 7th Marines,

Vital close air support. (Photo USMC)

dispatched a battalion to relieve his trapped men to the south. However, the Marines found it impossible to break through the strong Chinese positions that blocked their way. A similar attempt from Hagaru-ri also failed when a reinforced company encountered robust Chinese resistance on the road northward.

At midday, General Almond flew into the battle zone by helicopter to personally assess the desperate situation in which his corps had become entrapped by superior Chinese forces. After visiting General Smith at his US 1st Marine Division command post at Hagaru-ri, Almond flew to the north of the Changjin Reservoir to meet with Colonel Faith, commanding the US 1/32nd. Positioned on high ground above the Pungyuri inlet into the reservoir, 4 miles north-east of Colonel MacLean's US 31st Regiment, Faith's battalion had survived a difficult night. As mentioned earlier, at the inlet itself the US 3/31st and elements of the US 57th FAB had met a much different fate. Both battalion commanders had been wounded and the CPVA now held high ground commanding the American positions. Bizarrely, and fully aware that units of the US 1st Marine and US 7th divisions were caught in isolated pockets around the Changjin Reservoir, Almond endorsed MacLean's plans to resume the Yalu offensive the moment reinforcements were received. MacLean interpreted the almost fatal Chinese onslaught during the night as being last-ditch efforts by dregs of fleeing CPVA divisions. At Hagaru-ri, where he held the strategically vital road junction, General Smith focused only on one immediate crisis: the withdrawal of his two Marine regiments to the north.

Elsewhere, tactical efforts concentrated on opening the main supply route, which included patrols, air reconnaissance and airstrikes. At 1.30 p.m. on 28 November, elements of D Company, US 2/1st Marines, left Koto-ri on a motorized patrol with the objective of clearing the road through to Hagaru-ri. After only 1,500 yards, the company came under small-arms and mortar fire from a ridge line to the east of the road. Two platoons were ordered to engage the Chinese while artillery was called in and airstrikes conducted. By mid-afternoon, the whole of D Company found itself in a major firefight with the well-entrenched Chinese position estimated at battalion strength. The Americans, unable to dislodge the Chinese, were ordered to return to their defensive perimeter positions. A platoon from F Company assisted with the medical evacuation of D Company dead and wounded: five killed and twenty-nine wounded.

With the road between Koto-ri and Hagaru-ri remaining firmly in enemy hands, by nightfall several infantry, Marine and support convoys were forced to harbour within

Communist SU-76 tank destroyer and an M26 heavy tank of the US 1st Marine Division. (Photo NARA)

the Koto-ri perimeter: HQ and B and C companies, US 185th Engineers Battalion; 41 (Independent) Commando, Royal Marines; G Company, US 3/1st Marines; Reconnaissance Company, US 1st Marine Division; and elements of E Company, US 1st Medical Battalion, US 31st Regiment; and Advance Command Group, US 1st Marine Division.

With the arrival late morning, 29 November, of B and D companies, US 1st Tank Battalion, a composite convoy was assembled to break out and get to Hagaru-ri. To the south of Koto-ri, a convoy of six trucks was ambushed in the Funchilin Pass, resulting in an overturned truck loaded with 4.2-inch mortar bombs being abandoned. The command post at Chinhŭng-ni was shortly able to ascertain that the truck had been captured by the CPVA.

At Koto-ri, at 8.35 p.m., Third Platoon, B Company, US 1st Tank Battalion, limped back into the perimeter with only four of their seven tanks with which they had tried to reach Hagaru-ri. Ten trucks were also left behind when the tank company commander had been ordered to return to Koto-ri.

At around 10 p.m., the B Company tank commander, blocked by stalled vehicles on the road, radioed an urgent appeal for infantry support. He was informed, however, that the Koto-ri defence perimeter could not be weakened and support would therefore not be forthcoming. Eventually, artillery support allowed the B Company tanks to return to Koto-ri, bringing with them their dead and wounded.

Shortly before 1 a.m., 29 November, Hagaru-ri came under fresh attack, the CPVA striking at the H Company sector and the roadblock to the south. The attack rapidly spread out along the entire southern front. On the perimeter left flank, I Company came under heavy enemy attack, with well-positioned high-explosive and white-phosphorus mortar fire dropping on the Americans for the rest of the night. But the position held, and ground lost during the night was regained with the assistance of air support.

That evening, remnants of the Task Force Drysdale column arrived from Koto-ri. Half of the Royal Marine commando force had become casualties, while G Company, US 3/1st Marines had sustained more than fifty killed and wounded.

The situation continued to deteriorate during 30 November as significantly increased Chinese forces threatened to overwhelm the entire main supply route from Chinhŭng-ni to Yudam-ni. Throughout the day, airstrikes and American artillery and mortar fire pounded Chinese positions to the north, west, east, north-east and south-east of Koro-ri. Stragglers from the previous day's convoy to Hagaru-ri continued to trickle back into the perimeter. Only one officer and sixty-nine other ranks from B Company, US 31st, made it back—the rest of the company being unaccounted for.

At Hagaru-ri, while G Company, US 3/31st, successfully regained high ground on the north-east sector, elements of the US 31st command group arrived from the north-east, reporting that the rest of the unit would probably arrive under cover of darkness.

Over forty-eight hours, the long stretch of road between Koto-ri and Hagaru-ri, dubbed 'Hell Fire Valley', had been a cauldron of pitched battles between the Chinese and UN forces, the latter with Marine Corsairs air support.

A wounded chaplain reads
a memorial service over the
snow-covered bodies of dead
Marines, Koto-ri. (Photo NARA)

The other part of Task Force Drysdale had become trapped in Hell Fire Valley. Under intense small-arms and mortar fire, the US 1st Marine Division's assistant G4 (logistics), Lieutenant Colonel A. Arthur Chidester, ordered the convoy to turn around and head back to Koto-ri. At that moment a mortar hit the ammunition truck, creating an inferno that blocked the way south. Around 140 soldiers, including most of B Company, US 31st, were trapped. Major James K. Eagen immediately set about organizing defences when he was wounded and captured by the CPVA. Chidester then also suffered severe wounds, causing him to relinquish command to Major John McLaughlin.

The Chinese attack increased in momentum during the night, inflicting major casualties on McLaughlin's rapidly shrinking enclave. By 3 a.m., the major's combat capability was down to forty men. Less than two hours later, McLaughlin capitulated, yielding to Chinese demands for his surrender. As they were marched north, the Hell Fire Valley captives were joined by other prisoners from the Changjin zone, until they numbered about three hundred. Colonel Chidester succumbed to his wounds; his remains were not recovered, and he was presumed dead in January 1954.

Thus ended Task Force Drysdale's three-day ordeal. Out of the original 922 men that set off from Koto-ri, 321 had become casualty statistics: 61 British Royal Marine commandos, 141 US Marines and 119 US infantry. A total of seventy-five vehicles, including tanks, were lost.

6. MACARTHUR'S DUNKIRK

Screaming, whistling, bugle-playing, Banzai-yelling 'Gooks'—
Like raving lunatics doing a demented Morris dance—
Reminding me of fireflies on a balmy summer's night,
Thrashed the obscene loops and strands of barbed-wire ignominy;
Halting long enough to be stilled by the Fusiliers Brens and Vickers.

One Time Out of History's Calendar'
Ashley Cunningham-Boothe
Royal Northumberland Fusiliers[*]

By the beginning of December 1950, General MacArthur's grand design for a 'home-by-Christmas' pincer victory achieved by General Walker's US Eighth Army on the left and General Almond's US X Corps on the right, lay in tatters across the Korean peninsula. At great cost of troops and equipment, the Yalu River offensive had, in the space of a few days, become a series of disastrous defeats across the whole UN front in North Korea. Isolated pockets of troops, enveloped by screaming CPVA soldiers blowing whistles and bugles, fought to the death as successive rescue attempts also failed at unsustainable cost. It would become an enormous operation of escape and withdrawal, the likes of which had not been seen since the beaches of Dunkirk in June 1940.

To the east of the Changjin Reservoir, with Colonel MacLean missing in action, Colonel Faith assumed command of the US 31st. All Faith could do was to dig in and await rescue. Airdrops and constant Marine airstrikes prevented the position from being overrun. However, radio communications with Hagaru-ri were poor and Faith had the added responsibility of keeping 500 wounded American and South Korean troops alive. Then, 4 miles south of Faith's perimeter, the US 31st Tank Company that had been trying to reach Faith, was withdrawn. Whilst further reducing Faith's odds of survival, the armour had kept a possible escape route open for the beleaguered American infantry regiment.

During the night of 30 November, the CPVA attack continued unabated, resulting in a further 100 wounded. The exhausted Faith, accepting now that his situation was untenable, at first light on 1 December began preparations for a breakout at midday. Heavy ordnance was rendered unserviceable and the wounded loaded onto trucks.

Delayed by the late arrival of air support, which also accidentally dropped napalm on the head of the regiment's column, by 3 p.m., Faith had only covered 2 miles. Here, at the bottom of Hill 1221, the column was stalled at a destroyed bridge. For the next two hours,

---

[*] Ashley Cunningham-Boothe and Peter Farrar, Eds., *British Forces in the Korean War* (British Korean Veterans Association, Halifax, 1997).

US Marine column waits in appalling winter conditions. (Photo USMC)

as the trucks were laboriously winched across the icy stream, heavy CPVA machine-gun fire peppered the column, resulting in heavy casualties, especially among the vulnerable wounded in the trucks.

After only moving a few hundred yards, the column came across a heavily fortified CPVA roadblock. Incredibly, after launching several determined attacks, Faith broke through, but not before he was hit in the chest by shrapnel from a Chinese grenade. Heading south in the dark, the column continued to take machine-gun fire and phosphorus grenades. Some of the trucks overturned, crushing those inside. The column was now abandoned and several hundred survivors staggered across the frozen Changjin in the direction of Hagaru-ri. The Chinese let them go.

The wounded Colonel Faith was placed in the cab of a Deuce and a Half truck, but as they passed through the remaining CPVA roadblock—the last truck to do so—Faith was fatally hit by small-arms fire.* The driver was able to escape into the dark to find his

---

* In September 2004, Colonel Faith's remains were among some of the last the North Koreans allowed to be removed from that country. At a burial spot near the Changjin Reservoir, members of the Joint Prisoners of War/Missing in Action, Accounting Command (JPAC), recovered remains of American troops, which were taken to JPAC's Central Identification Laboratory, at Joint Base Pearl/Hickam, Hawaii, for identification. In a time-consuming analysis, on 14 August 2012, positive DNA matches from family samples identified 19 of the 101 bones to be those of Colonel Faith.

way to Hagaru-ri. The 32-year-old Lieutenant Colonel Don Carlos Faith was posthumously awarded the Medal of Honor. The citation, in part, reads:

> Assuming command [replacing missing in action Colonel MacLean] of the force his unit had joined he was given the mission of attacking to join friendly elements to the south. Lieutenant Colonel Faith, although physically exhausted in the bitter cold, organized and launched an attack which was soon stopped by enemy fire. He ran forward under enemy small-arms and automatic weapons fire, got his men on their feet and personally led the fire attack as it blasted its way through the enemy ring. As they came to a hairpin curve, enemy fire from a roadblock again pinned the column down.
>
> Lieutenant Colonel Faith organized a group of men and directed their attack on the enemy positions on the right flank. He then placed himself at the head of another group of men and in the face of direct enemy fire led an attack on the enemy roadblock, firing his pistol and throwing grenades. When he had reached a position approximately 30 yards from the roadblock he was mortally wounded, but continued to direct the attack until the roadblock was overrun.
>
> Throughout the five days of action Lieutenant Colonel Faith gave no thought to his safety and did not spare himself. His presence each time in the position of greatest danger was an inspiration to his men. Also, the damage he personally inflicted firing from his position at the head of his men was of material assistance on several occasions. Lieutenant Colonel Faith's outstanding gallantry and noble self-sacrifice above and beyond the call of duty reflect the highest honor on him and are in keeping with the highest traditions of the U.S. Army.[*]

Over the following two days, the pathetic remnants of the US 31st Regiment trickled into the Hagaru-ri perimeter. The CPVA returned the severely wounded among the prisoners, while rescue parties, under fire, recovered more. One such patrol discovered 300 dead in the destroyed and abandoned trucks at Hundong-ni. Over four days, Task Force Faith lost half its strength dead or taken prisoner—a profound sacrifice that stalled the 80th Division, CPVA XXVII Corps long enough to save the Marines at Hagaru-ri from a similar fate.

On 30 November, General Almond finally broke off the US X Corps's Yalu offensive and issued orders for the evacuation of Yudam-ni. The next night, a battalion of Marines jumped off from Yudam-ni to march on Fox Hill where Captain Barber had, with the assistance of airdrops, been able to withstand repeated Chinese attacks. Fighting the enemy and the cold all the way, Fox Hill was reached on 2 December. At last, the badly wounded, stretcher-borne Barber and 86 of the original F Company's strength of 237, were able to leave Fox Hill. The only officer not wounded, Lieutenant John Dunne, First Platoon, assumed command.

---

[*] Department of the Army General Order No. 59, 2 August 1951.

Evacuation from Yudam-ni. (Photo USMC)

From 1 December, the US 5th and 7th Marines commenced evacuating Yudam-ni south toward Hagaru-ri. Lieutenant Colonel Raymond G. Davis, US 1/7th Marines, led 800 armed walking wounded and more than 1,000 truck-borne wounded and frostbitten down the main supply route. Such was the decimation of D and E companies, that the two were merged to form what was referred to as 'Dog Easy' Company. Morale could not have been lower.

As the two Marine regiments neared the Hagaru-ri perimeter, the column stopped momentarily to form up into something that resembled an orderly, marching column of troops. However, an observer among the many welcoming the Marines, summed up the tragedy that stumbled in from the frozen darkness:

Those slightly wounded helped one another, grinding their teeth and advancing in heavy steps, their M-1 rifles hanging disorderly on them. The accompanying vehicles were fully loaded with seriously wounded unconscious soldiers. Some were simply tied to the radiators of the vehicles. They were frozen like pieces of hard wood. Their bodies were covered by fragments of pink frozen blood.*

---

* Stanley Weintraub, *A Christmas Far from Home: An Epic Tale of Courage and Survival during the Korean War* (Hachette, UK, 2014).

B-26 Invaders on a bombing run over North Korea, October 1951. (Photo USAF)

In the western US Eighth Army sector, the unusual and high-risk deployment of Martin B-26 Invader light bombers of the US Fifth Air Force had saved units of the US 25th Division from likely destruction as Major General William B. Kean withdrew south.

On 27 November, the British 29th (Independent) Infantry Brigade Group (British 29th) received orders to join US I Corps, commanded by Major General Frank W. Milburn. Two days later, the brigade completed its first long-distance move by being trucked 80 miles from Kaesong to P'yŏngyang. On arrival, brigade group commander Major General Thomas Brodie was ordered to move north to Sukch'ŏn to conduct line of communication duties in support of the US Eighth Army's drive on the Yalu River. However, upon reaching Sukch'ŏn, there were already indications of 'the general exodus southwards which had started in a small way as soon as it had arrived in SUKCHON'.*

The brigade group moved back to P'yŏngyang tasked with defending the northern approaches and bridges over the Taedong River, acting as a rear guard while the remainder of Walker's forces in the western sector retreated. The North Korean capital was abandoned on 5 December and the Taedong bridges blown the following day.

---

* WO 308/85 War Office (Korea) National Archives, London.

For the remainder of the year, the British 29th was held in US I Corps reserve a few miles north of Seoul.

Arguably, the US 2nd Division might also have fallen to the CPVA had the JOC not given Major General Laurence B. Keiser's division priority when processing air-support requests. In one day alone, the US 38th Regiment received thirty-eight air-support sorties.

With the completion of the US 2nd Division's bloody and costly evacuation south, the US Eighth Army largely lost contact with the Chinese invaders, a relative respite that would last several weeks. Commander General Walker had initially intended to hold a defensive line along the trans-peninsula road from P'yŏngyang to Wŏnsan. However, the speed at which the CPVA XVIII Corps advanced denied Walker sufficient time to make a stand.

By mid-December, the US Eighth Army had regrouped and was concentrated along an axis extending from the Kumpo Peninsula on the west coast to Chŏksŏng near the Imjin River north of Seoul. It was Walker's plan to fight a delaying action in defence of the South Korean capital.

In the US X Corps sector, the situation was far more desperate. With the overextended troops on the mountains of east Korea facing dangerous prospects for survival, General Earle E. Partridge, commander of the US Fifth Air Force in Korea and Japan, committed the US 1st Marine Air Wing to exclusively provide the corps with air support. All requests for assistance from the ground would bypass the JOC and be channelled directly to the Marine air unit. Following a personal visit to Hŭngnam on 1 December, General Partridge placed his whole light-bomber capacity at the US X Corps' disposal. In Tokyo, US Far East Air Force commander General George E. Stratemeyer made the entire medium-bomber force available to General Almond to employ in whatever manner required.

In the last few days of November, the FEAF Combat Cargo Command was stretched to the limit with airdrop sorties to keep beleaguered units at Yudam-ni and Sinhung-ni alive. Operating out of Wŏnsan, C-47s of US 21st Troop Carrier Squadron (US 21st Squadron) dropped twenty-six tons of ammunition to the cut-off Marines and GIs. On 29 November, General Almond requested airdrops of 400 tons of air supply, a logistically impossible task for the US 21st Squadron. The reality was that Combat Cargo could only manage seventy tons a day across the entire operation.

At Ashiya in Japan, the closest American airfield to Korea, and since September 1950 operational base to C-54 Skymasters and C-119 Flying Boxcars of the US 314th Troop Carrier group, round-the-clock packaging of weapons, ammunition, petroleum products, rations, winter clothing and general essential supplies commenced. At Hamhŭng, a short distance to the north-west of the east coast port of Hŭngnam on the main supply route to Hagaru-ri, a quartermaster supply-packing unit was established at the Y'onp'o Airfield (K-27). From Tokyo, commander of Combat Cargo, General William H. Tunner, received orders to commit all his C-46s (Curtis Commandos), C-47s and C-119s in support of the US X Corps. At this time, seven Douglas DC-3s of the 13th Hellenic Flight (squadron), the Royal Hellenic Air Force, supplemented the massive airdrop operation, flying thirty sorties to Hagaru-ri.

Above: Arming a Douglas AD-4 Skyraider, USS *Philippine Sea* (CV-47). (Photo US Navy)

Below: US 314th Troop Carrier Group C-119 'Flying Boxcar'. (Photo NARA)

While his troops battled their way back from Yudam-ni, at Hagaru-ri General Smith had engineers working non-stop around the clock to dig a semblance of an airstrip in the frozen ground. The crude, short landing strip would, however, not be able to accommodate any aircraft larger than the ubiquitous, twin-propeller Douglas C-47 Skytrain.

On 1 December, the first C-47 landed at the unfinished airfield at Hagaru-ri. Over the next five days, USAF and Marine aircraft and crew uplifted more than 4,300 medical cases, many suffering from severe frostbite. Personnel of the US 801st Medical Air Evacuation Squadron were responsible for the care and transfer of all medical evacuees. At the same time, incoming aircraft shuttled in 530 Marine replacements, food, ammunition and medical supplies.

Meanwhile at Koto-ri, corpsmen of the US 2/1st Marines also prepared a patch of rocky, frozen ground that was an airstrip in name only. By 10 December, 240 sorties had been conducted into the two rudimentary airfields, evacuating almost 4,700 wounded and sick troops while delivering 274 tons of supplies.

There was now a notable reduction in CPVA frontal attacks of the Hagaru-ri perimeter. Emulating the tactics of their comrades against the US 2nd Division south of Kunu-ri, the 76th and 77th divisions, CPVA XXVI Corps, started to concentrate on the movement of Marines as they withdrew to the south. During the afternoon of 3 December, tank and infantry patrols from the US 3/1st Marines ventured northward in an attempt to locate friendly troops. Unsuccessful, the patrols were called back at 6 p.m. For the first time, the Chinese did not attack during the night.

An hour later, the lead elements of the awaited stragglers made it to the relative safety of Hagaru-ri and much-needed food and shelter. The amorphous miscellany of survivors from the eastern shores of Changjin Reservoir were reorganized as a provisional regiment under a reconstituted US 31st Infantry Regiment. The unit was placed under US 1st Marine Division command and disposed in a section of the defensive perimeter.

At Chinhŭng-ni the US 1/1st Marines continued to improve perimeter defences, while equipment and supplies not essential for defence purposes were transferred to Hamhŭng.

To the north, the US 2/1st Marines at Koto-ri hosted General Almond on a visit to award medals to nine Marines. CPVA attacks were described a 'of relatively light intensity ... intermittently from the north'.*

On 4 December, while 'friendly troops' continued to arrive from the north, airstrikes persisted throughout the day on targets of opportunity around Hagaru-ri. At 2.30 p.m., the remainder of the 41st Royal Marines and a platoon of D Company tanks set off on the Yudam-ni road on a mission to either retrieve or destroy abandoned American artillery on the road. Four 155mm field pieces were discovered to have already been destroyed and another four of similar calibre rendered unserviceable.

---

* *1st Marine Division Special Action Diary – October 1950–December 1950.* (National Archives and Records Administration, College Park Maryland).

A US 1st Marine memorial service at the division's cemetery at Hamhung, Korea, following the break-out from Changjin Reservoir. (Photo USMC)

Over the next two days, the medical evacuation of personnel by air from Hagaru-ri and Koto-ri continued, while respective defence perimeters, with close air support, remained firm. On 6 December, all available aircraft covered the withdrawal south of the US 7th Marines from Hagaru-ri. A few hours earlier, General Smith and members of his divisional staff arrived by helicopter at Koto-ri from Hagaru-ri.

Throughout 7 December, the troops from Hagaru-ri arrived at Koto-ri, including the US 5th and 7th Marines and the composite elements of the US 31st. By 11 p.m., the withdrawal from Hagaru-ri was complete and all troops secure in the defence perimeter. In preparation for the massive evacuation of troops and equipment, General Smith would spend the night planning the clearance of all enemy forces from the main supply route between the two concentration points. His command post had also received a signal from US X Corps to the east stating that the US 3/7th would be arriving at Chinhŭng-ni to relieve the US 1/1st Marines.

In a blinding snowstorm in which visibility was reduced to six feet, before daylight on 8 December, at Chinhŭng-ni the US 1/1st Marines jumped off north along the main supply route. With Hill 1081 as its objective, positions along the route were established by C Company, then B Company, while A Company moved on Hill 1081. Encountering enemy forces all the way, by nightfall the three companies were short of their objective and were forced to dig in for the night.

At the same time, the US 7th Marines advanced south from Koto-ri on assigned divisional objectives. A battalion of US 5th Marines jumped off next, while the other two battalions extended the defensive perimeter to the south of the US 2/31st and the northern sector between D and companies, US 2/1st Marines. Having been relieved from their defence positions by H and I companies, US 3/1st Marines, elements of the US 185th Engineers and C Company, US 1st Engineers, prepared to blow up ammunition and supplies which could not be loaded onto trucks. In what would become a flood of petrified humans, some 3,000 refugees had already gathered at the northern roadblock. The American defenders resorted to gunfire to drive them back.

The next morning—9 December—airstrikes and artillery fire prepared the crest of Hill 1081 for an A Company assault. However, the CPVA were well entrenched, clinging stubbornly to their commanding position. It would be 3 p.m. before A Company took the hill, but with heavy casualties. At Koto-ri, the 41st Royal Marines relieved the US 3/1st Marines as the latter prepared to withdraw.

By 11 December, and facing relatively light Chinese resistance, in an enormous perpetual movement the UN forces made Chinhŭng-ni, then Majŏn-dong for onward trucking to an assembly area between Hamhung and Chigyŏng. Facing constant CPVA harassment, the withdrawal was not without incident and casualties. At 11 p.m. the previous night, about 3 miles south of the top of Funchilin Pass, the tail end of a Reconnaissance Company, US 1st Marines Division, and US 1st Tank Battalion column came under heavy CPVA attack. Sustaining casualties and under threat of being overrun by CPVA soldiers moving with the refugees, seven tanks were abandoned. With no hope—or intention—of recovery, the abandoned armour was destroyed by air the next morning.

The last of the Marines and infantry boarded trucks at 11.30 a.m. Most of the troops had marched non-stop for more than twenty hours in adverse weather conditions. Lugging their packs, personal weapons and sleeping bags, the troops had covered 22 miles.

Early in December, Tokyo officially ordered the withdrawal of all UN forces from North Korea in what would be one of the largest military and refugee evacuation missions in American history.

Such was the speed of the US Eighth Army's southward movement, that there was a risk of the North Korean west coast port of Chinnamp'o becoming exposed before evacuation could take place. To avoid yet another disaster, Vice Admiral C. Turner Joy commander of US Naval forces, Far East, despatched other naval units under Rear Admiral Lyman A. Thackrey, including British, Canadian and Australian vessels, to organize the evacuation of UN forces from Chinnamp'o and Inch'ŏn.

Task Group 90.1, comprising the attack transport (APA) vessels *Bayfield*, *Bexar* and *Okanogan*, and the attack cargo (AKA) vessels *Algol* and *Montague*, sailed independently from Japan for the Yellow Sea. For protection, six west coast destroyers of TE 95.12 were placed on standby for escort duties, while HMS *Ceylon* sailed from Sasebo in Japan.

Korean refugees clamber onto anything that floats as UN forces evacuate Hŭngnam. (Photo NARA)

Recalled from Hong Kong to Sasebo, Vice-Admiral Bill Andrewes, Royal Navy, was preparing to sail with the carrier HMS *Theseus* and four destroyers for the west coast.

As most of the UN forces made their way south in vehicles or on foot, the outloading mission at Chinnamp'o was completed from 4 to 6 December. At Inch'ŏn, through December and into early January 1951, Admiral Thackrey's ships outloaded 69,000 troops, 64,000 North Korean refugees, 1,000 refugees and more than 55,000 tons of cargo.

The evacuation of UN forces on the east coast was logistically considerably more demanding, compounded by mounting pressure from the CPVA to push the withdrawing UN forces into the Sea of Japan. Whilst it was reliably estimated that it would take ten days to evacuate the US X Corps, there was no certainty in General Almond's mind that the closing Chinese forces would allow him that much time. Evacuation by air—both land- and carrier-based—would have to complement the naval effort to the maximum. At Yŏnp'o, there would be a tight four-day window to utilize the airstrip before US X Corps protection was withdrawn on the morning of 17 December. In an intensive operation, Combat Cargo Command set up a twenty-four-hour operation, centred on the US 1st Troop Carrier Group (Provisional) with aircraft taking off at five-minute intervals. By the end

Supplies and equipment await outloading at Hŭngnam. (Photo NARA)

of the operation, 393 C-119 Flying Boxcar sorties were flown from Yŏnp'o, transporting 228 medical evacuees, 3,890 passengers and almost 2,100 tons of cargo.

The vast bulk of the US X Corps east coast evacuation would be by sea. From the various assembly stages, the massed UN troops of the US X Corps would be moved to the transit beaches at Hŭngnam, Wŏnsan and Sŏngjin. With the Marines concentrated just inland from Hŭngnam, the US 7th Division had been ordered to withdraw from the Manchurian border to Hamhŭng.

Farther north up the coast, the ROKA I Corps was ordered to retire on the port of Sŏngjin. A mining and timber export centre, the harbour facilities, including a 1,800-foot quay, allowed for a textbook recovery that ended on 9 December. Heading the task force was USS *Noble* (APA-218), a Haskell-class attack transport commanded by Captain Michael F. Flaherty. Included were two merchantmen from Wŏnsan, a Shipping Control Authority for the Japanese Merchant Marine (SCAJAP) vessel, a South Korean LST, and the Allen M. Sumner-class destroyers USS *Maddox* and USS *Moore*.

Meanwhile, at Wŏnsan the outloading of the remains of the US 3rd Division remained on schedule. Elements of the USMC rendered onshore assistance, while a battalion

Offshore at Wŏnsan, the USS *Saint Paul* (CA-73) provides covering fire for the evacuation. (Photo US Navy)

of GIs and two of South Korean marines maintained a defensive perimeter. Offshore, the USS *Saint Paul* (CA-73), a Baltimore-class cruiser commanded by Vice Admiral Roscoe H. Hillenkoetter, the Allen M. Sumner-class destroyers USS *Zellars* (DD-777) and USS *Hank* (DD-702), and the USS *Sperry* (AS-12), a Fulton-class submarine tender, provided covering fire when the beachhead came under threat.

With the exception of a ROKA marine battalion tasked to cover the removal of Marine Air Group 12 (MAG 12) from Kalma Pondo, Wŏnsan was cleared of UN forces by 7 December. All that remained was an empty Victory ship, a class of Second World War cargo vessel. With the naval element providing covering fire, North Korean refugees on the beach were allowed to embark. The loading, way in excess of the ship's capacity, was completed during the hours of darkness of 9 December. The next morning, as the last transport cleared the harbour, Admiral Hillenkoetter took the *Saint Paul* and the *Hank* back north to augment naval cover fire at Hŭngnam. The total Wŏnsan lift numbered 3,800 troops, 7,000 refugees, 1,150 vehicles and 10,000 tons of supplies.

Now, only sixty days after the heavy price the US Navy had paid—70 per cent of the casualties sustained during the Korean war and the loss of four vessels—to land the US 1st Marine Division at Wŏnsan, the only remaining activity in the deserted harbour was a salvage operation. With the high-speed transport USS *Diachenko* (APD-123) in charge and *Zellars* and *Sperry* providing cover, the rescue vessel USS *Conserver* (ARS-39) was sending divers down to attempt the recovery of classified equipment on the wrecks of the sunken US Navy minesweepers USS *Pirate* (AM 275) and USS *Pledge* (AM 277). Both vessels had gone down, with the loss of twelve lives, after detonating mines during clearing operations to provide the Marines with a safe passage through the outer harbour to the beaches only weeks earlier. After several unsuccessful attempts, the grim decision was made to blow up the two vessels.

At Hŭngnam, by 14 December seven chartered merchant vessels and a miscellany of transports and landing ships had loaded the Marines and sailed for Pusan. Outloading now commenced on the US 7th Division. To keep the east coast route secure during the evacuation operations, an amphibious landing comprising 25,000 South Korean troops and 700 vehicles was executed at Mukho to the south.

All the while, the CPVA capitalized on the withdrawal of UN forces along the main supply route the whole distance from Yudam-ni to the coast. Carrier air operations and jet combat air patrols and sorties were maintained over Hŭngnam and inland along the road to retard the Chinese advance on the port. On 15 December, the USS *Saint Paul* started to lay down 8-inch fire for deep support and interdiction on CPVA movements. Two days later, the USS *Rochester* took over the 8-inch shelling in conjunction with the flat-trajectory fire from on-station cruisers and destroyers. On 21 December, three rocket ships commenced firing on hills on the eastern flank. An AKA, an LST and the cargo ship USS *Ryer* (AKL-9) operated an ammunition-replenishment shuttle service out of the harbour to the ships participating in the onshore barrage. During the evacuation phase, 18,637 5-inch and 2,932 8-inch rounds were discharged, 70 and 27 per cent more than that expended during the Inch'ŏn landing of 15 September.

Around midday on 19 December, General Almond and his US X Corps staff boarded the USS *Mount McKinley*, relinquishing command of ground forces to Major General Robert H. Soule, commander of the US 3rd Division. Admiral Doyle assumed responsibility for the defence of Hŭngnam. At dawn on 21 December, the convoy with the outloaded US 7th Division sailed south.

Three regimental combat teams with support artillery, six battalions of artillery and three anti-aircraft battalions remained in the town to hold a defensive perimeter that had been squeezed by the Chinese down to a radius of 5,000 yards. The date for the conclusion of the evacuation of Hŭngnam was set for 24 December.

Outloading of the US 3rd Division commenced on 22 December, leaving the troops and their artillery until last. Combat missions and air support sorties from the carrier strike force TF-77 increased by more than 50 per cent on the 23rd. The USS *Missouri* arrived the same day as the last American artillery battalion embarked.

US Navy high-speed transport USS *Begor* (APD-127) departing Hŭnungnam as UN forces blow up the port infrastructure, 24 December 1950. (Photo NARA)

At 11 a.m. the following day, the last of the corps troops embarked, and shortly after 2 p.m., Admiral Doyle gave the order for explosive charges to be detonated to destroy the harbour infrastructure. The final withdrawal by sea of UN forces from Hŭngnam, with the utilization of more than 190 naval and merchant vessels, amounted to 105,000 American and South Korean troops, 91,000 refugees, 17,500 vehicles and 350,000 tons of cargo.

7. THE SACRED STRUGGLE

When it comes to courage, which of you can separate the stupid from the brave?
How can we take away from one soldier—
Because he serves the other side—
That which we would see as being nothing less than heroic in our own;
In battles so intense and infamous as to earn themselves a place in history,
Joining Battle Honours on a Regiment's Colours.
God forbid that you should spend one day of your life with the 'Shitdiggers'
  of the Infantry, writing history!

'One Time Out of History's Calendar'
Ashley Cunningham-Boothe
Royal Northumberland Fusiliers*

In the corridors of power in Washington, finger-pointing was the order of the day to apportion or transfer blame for the Korean debacle in November and December 1950: poor intelligence, General Douglas MacArthur's disdain of authority, President Harry S. Truman for personally failing to control the UN forces commander.

MacArthur now developed a concern for the safety of Japan, prompting him to ask the Joint Chiefs of Staff (JCS) for reinforcements for the country's defence. With resources already stretched, the JCS contemplated a complete withdrawal from the Korean peninsula, a view reflected in a 29 December directive giving the security of Japan and the UN Command priority over South Korea. Included were instructions for retiring defensive positions down the peninsula, while inflicting as much damage as possible on the CPVA forces.

Commander of the US Eighth Army, General Walton Walker, had already been planning such a contingency on MacArthur's request. Walker had drawn four lines of defence: 'Able', north of P'yŏngyang, 'Baker', along the Imjin River and the 38th Parallel, 'Charlie', around Seoul and in a line to the east coast via Hongch'ŏn and, finally, 'Dog', on a P'yŏngt'aek–Wŏnju–Samch'ŏk west–east axis.

However, fate dictated that the 61-year-old veteran of two world wars, lauded for his mobile defence of the Pusan Perimeter, would not live to implement his plans. On 23 December, while travelling to Ŭijŏngbu to visit troops, a civilian truck crashed into his jeep. He was rushed to a US 24th Division clearing station, where staff pronounced him dead from multiple head injuries. Lieutenant General Matthew B. Ridgway,

---

* Ashley Cunningham-Boothe and Peter Farrar, Eds., *British Forces in the Korean War* (British Korean Veterans Association, Halifax, 1997).

General Matthew B. Ridgway, centre, and staff in Korea. (Photo NARA)

an accomplished veteran of Second World War airborne forces command, replaced Walker as commander of the US Eighth Army.

In spite of the heavy cost of pushing the UN forces out of North Korea—the USMC estimated the CPVA Third Field Army alone suffered 72,000 casualties—Mao Zedong was determined to maintain the initiative and cross the 38th Parallel and ordered Peng Dehuai to cut the 38th Parallel.

Far East Command intelligence had, by this time, established reliable estimates of Chinese forces poised across the peninsula. Facing the US Eighth Army was the CPVA Fourth Field Army, comprising the XXXVIII, XXXIX, XL, XLII, L and LXVI corps and totalling 177,000 troops. A new development was the rapid revitalization of under-strength North Korean rifle divisions assembled from survivors of battles in South Korea and recruits from training schools along the Yalu. The KPA I Corps, with a strength of 14,100 troops, was disposed at the left of the Chinese field army, while 24,000 men of the KPA II and V corps faced South Korean units in central Korea. However, Peng would rely on the 102,000 troops CPVA Third Field Army, comprising the XX, XXVI and XXVII corps, to advance south and west from Hŭngnam to cover his left flank.

On 31 December 1950, the CPVA launched the third offensive of its Korean campaign. Typically, the Chinese adhered to their tactic of waging war in the hours of darkness, with artillery and mortar fire preceding the blowing of whistles and bugles that galvanized thousands of Mao's peasant soldiers. The US 24th and 25th divisions being the prime objective, the American artillery inflicted major casualties on the enemy but failed to stem the determined attack.

As dawn broke, the CPVA had penetrated the line between the two divisions, hitting the ROKA 1st and 6th divisions holding that sector. To the east of Seoul, the Chinese broke through the UN forces' defence line, threatening to encircle the city. General Ridgway immediately implemented the plan to establish a bridgehead around Seoul by pulling back the US I and IX corps, consisting of ten infantry regiments, several hundred tanks and fifteen artillery battalions equipped with 150mm, 105mm and 8-inch howitzers. As the two corps withdrew in a generally orderly manner, the only major incident occurred when the CPVA overran companies of the 1st Battalion, Royal Ulster Rifles (1/RUR), British 29th, at 'Happy Valley', Chaegunghyon. During the night of 3/4 January, while covering the withdrawal of UN forces to the south of the Han River, 1RUR came under heavy enemy fire, which degenerated into a melee of close-quarter fighting. The next day, the casualty return listed 208 killed, wounded and missing in action, a figure that was subsequently reduced to 157 upon the return of wounded and missing to the battalion.

With the exception of the new troop dispositions around Seoul, defence Line Charlie passed along the south bank of the Han River before extending to the east coast from Yangp'yŏng. At P'yŏngt'aek, 40 miles to the south on the west coast, Line Dog ran across the peninsula to Wŏonp'o-ri.

On 4 January 1951, Seoul was abandoned, followed by Inch'ŏn the next day, with bridges and infrastructure blown up as the UN forces withdrew. By 6 January, the US Eighth Army had completed its move to Line Dog.

A week later, the JCS issued a new directive from Washington, calling on the UN forces to hold their current dispositions, albeit with the knowledge that this would be transient at best. At the United Nations, intense diplomatic consultations sought to secure a ceasefire in Korea. A UN-approved administration of a unified Korea in exchange for negotiations over the future of Formosa (Taiwan) and Communist China's membership of the UN. Beijing, however, insisted that UN membership was a prerequisite to any talk of a cessation of hostilities on the peninsula.

While diplomatic initiatives reached an almost inevitable impasse, on 16 January, General Ridgway commenced probing reconnaissance missions—'Wolfhound'—as far as Suwŏn and Osan, followed by a counteroffensive move by the US Eighth Army nine days later, dubbed Operation Thunderbolt. Contact with the CPVA was light as the Chinese elected to retire north of the 38th Parallel. Emboldened, Ridgway commenced a two-division advance on the Han River. On the east coast, Operation Ascendant saw the US Navy's CTF 95 set sail on 29 January for an amphibious feint in the Kansŏng–Kosŏng area in support of the northward advance of South Korean units.

Elements of the US 9th Regiment north of Seoul. (Photo NARA)

By 11 February, elements of the ROKA Marines had reoccupied Inch'ŏn and the US I and IX corps had approached the south bank of the Han River where they inflicted heavy casualties on the CPVA L and XXXVIII corps.

On General Ridgway's right flank, a conglomerate of 10,000 Chinese troops, drawn from three CPVA corps and commanded by Wen Yucheng, moved on Wŏnju. Whilst breaching the ROKA line, the UN forces, including elements of the US 1st Marine Division, moved up from anti-guerrilla operations in the south, was able to repulse the Chinese. In what the Americans would refer to as the 'Wŏnju Shoot', the Chinese suffered 5,000 casualties, including the total annihilation of the 3rd Battalion, 359th Regiment, CPVA XXX Corps.

There can be no doubt that without air support from FEAF, the UN force may not have held its line from collapsing under pressure of the CPVA tidal wave. In the first five days in January 1951 as the Chinese launched the third offensive of their Korean campaign, the US Fifth Air Force flew just on 2,600 sorties, 60 per cent of which were against close-support targets. Thereafter, most of the air sorties comprised armed-reconnaissance strikes north of the Chinese lines.

In the opening stages of the latest CPVA surge, FEAF Bomber Command concentrated its efforts against hostile forces and supplies at P'yŏngyang. On 3 and 5 January, a total of 163 Boeing B-29 Superfortress heavy bombers saturated parts of the North Korean capital with incendiary bombs.

Concurrently, the fighter-bombers of the US Fifth Air Force and light bombers from the 452nd Wing were unrelenting in striking at the advancing CPVA, while at night Douglas B-26 Invader 'night-intruders' hit the Chinese forces at a time of day when they tended to be most active. The innovative employment of Mark VIII parachute flares, dropped by a C-47 'Lightning Bug', not only provided the light bombers with near-daylight visibility for target selection, but forced the enemy to break off contact in the knowledge that air attacks would accompany the flares.

Adverse weather conditions in the form of Siberian snowstorms moving south grounded US Fifth Air Force units on 10 January, allowing the CPVA to consolidate and strengthen their hold on Wŏnju, abandoned by the US 2nd Division a few days earlier. As the storms subsided on 11 January, FEAF Bomber Command and the US Fifth Air Force resumed support for US X Corps ground troops. Fighter-bombers hit CPVA columns moving on the US 2nd Division's flanks and others advancing south along the roads from Hongch'ŏn and Hoengsŏng. Over Wŏnju, B-29s from the US 98th Group, for the first time in operations dropped proximity-fused 500-pound general-purpose bombs. The air-bursting bombs carpeted the ground with lethal steel fragments.

The ongoing inability to effectively challenge American air superiority hastened China's training and equipping of its air arm at bases in Manchuria and rear bases. With an increase in the acquisition of MiG-15s from the Soviet Union, and combined with the withdrawal of Sabres over the Yalu, Chinese air activity over Sinŭiju increased as the command strived to enhance pilot combat experience.

This was evidenced on 21 January when twelve MiG-15s 'boxed' a flight of four Lockheed F-80 Shooting Stars, bringing down one of the slower American jets. Later the same day, sixteen MiGs fell on two flights of Republic F-84 Thunderjets from US 523rd Squadron that were dive-bombing a bridge straddling the Ch'ŏngch'ŏn River. One Thunderjet was shot down, while squadron commander Lieutenant Colonel William E. Bertram became the first Thunderjet pilot to destroy a MiG in air combat.

On 23 January, thirty-three Thunderjets from the US 27th Fighter-Escort Wing took off from Taegu on a mission to strafe the Sinŭiju airfield. Over the target, the Americans were engaged by thirty MiGs, resulting in a series of dogfights lasting almost half an hour. Afterwards, all the Thunderjets returned safely to base, claiming four kills, three probably destroyed and four damaged. The statistics reflected Chinese pilots' lack of combat experience.

However, the competition for control of Yalu airspace dropped off with the withdrawal south of UN forces. General Partridge continued with the redeployment of the US Fifth Air Force to their home bases in Japan, abandoning the Taegu airfield by the

Republic F-84E Thunderjet fighters over Korea. (Photo USAF)

end of January. During February, air combat over north-west Korea was avoided as the Chinese took hold of the skies over the area between the Ch'ŏngch'ŏn and Yalu rivers, a zone that earned the sobriquet 'MiG Alley' for the rest of the conflict. The Chinese would undertake an intense programme of airfield rehabilitation across the peninsula.

With the UN forces launching a counteroffensive as the CPVA broke off their third offensive, the US I Corps recaptured the Kimp'o Airfield on 10 February. Recognizing the opportunity to reassert his presence air force's presence, General Partridge ordered the repair of the landing grounds at Suwon, Kimp'o and Seoul, but to accommodate his jet fighters, this would take time.

Towards the end of February, the 334th Fighter-Interceptor Squadron, US 4th Wing, arrived at Taegu. However, the North American F-86 Sabres operating from Taegu had a limited range that meant they would be unable to operate north of P'yŏngyang.

On 1 March, delayed by unexpected headwinds, eighteen unescorted B-29s entered MiG Alley to bomb a bridge near Chongju. Intercepted by nine MiGs, ten of the bombers sustained damage, three seriously enough to require forced landings upon their return to Taegu. As a consequence, on 6 March, Sabres of US 334 Squadron were moved to Suwon for Yalu operational duties. In spite of the fact that the runway at Suwon was in a relatively poor state, during the month the American pilots went some way to restore a

North American F-86E Sabre of the US 334th Fighter-Interceptor Squadron. (Photo USAF)

balance of air power over the Yalu. Dogfights became more common, allowing bombers of the US 19th and 307th groups greater freedom of movement to execute interdiction raids in the area.

Regrouped and rested after the Hŭngnam evacuation, at Pusan the US X Corps was preparing to join the US Eighth Army on Line Dog. The corps still comprised the US 3rd and 7th divisions and the US 1st Marine Division, with the addition of the under-strength US 2nd Division.

To the east, a combined force of the US 23rd Regiment and the French Korea Battalion (*Battalion de Corée*), the latter commanded by French Foreign Legionnaire Lieutenant Colonel Magrin Vernerrey (nom de guerre Ralph Monclar), stubbornly hung onto Chip'yŏng-ni as 25,000 Chinese assailed their position. Only with the arrival of the US 1st Cavalry Division did the CPVA break off their attack.

Around the end of January to early February, General Lin Biao made the strategic decision to engage UN forces in 'protracted defensive battles', ordering his commanders to withdraw to strong defensive positions on the 38th Parallel. The CPVA L Corps would provide cover for rearguard action, allowing the CPVA Fourth Field Army to regroup and rest in preparation for a fresh offensive. Within days, Lin Biao would retire on medical grounds, to be succeeded by Peng Dehuai. Assuming command of a joint North Korean–Red Chinese forces headquarters, Peng took over control of all CPVA forces in Korea.

The new commander was equally adamant that the 38th Parallel must be held regardless of cost. A fourth offensive was being planned for May, but would be earlier if MacArthur's forces approached the 38th too closely.

With the withdrawal of the CPVA, General Ridgway launched Operation Killer on 18 February, moving the US IX and X corps north to clear the Wŏnju–Kangnŭng road and bring the centre abreast of the line to the west. By the end of the month, the Marines neared Hoengsŏng, the Killer objective, while on the Sea of Japan, Task Force 77 steamed north to execute a landing of South Korean marines on the island of Sin Do at Wŏnsan.

General Lin Biao had conceded that the CPVA third offensive had ended in failure, wanting it to be 'clearly understood that the failure of the Chinese offensive ... was due to the failure of the Chinese Central Government to furnish air and tank support as promised. If we had a strong air support, we could have driven the enemy into the sea'.[*]

During the first quarter of 1951, there was a growing desire in Washington and at Lake Success for the brokering of a ceasefire to allow for the pursuit of a solution to the Korean War. Both antagonists had suffered unsustainable losses and the UN objective of pushing the 'aggressor' back north of the 38th Parallel had largely been met.

However, supreme commander of UN forces in Korea, General Douglas MacArthur, continued to maintain that any enemy offensive had to be met with a stronger counteroffensive, and was therefore convinced that he should take the conflict to the CPVA by advancing north once more. The general envisaged east and west coast amphibious landings—including Nationalist Chinese forces—that would make Inch'ŏn and Wŏnsan small in comparison.

A proponent of the deployment of nuclear weapons, MacArthur also believed that a 5-mile-deep radioactive cobalt belt south of the Yalu would cut off the CPVA lines of supply and communication with Manchuria. Thereafter, the Chinese armies should be pursued into China where local industry had to be destroyed. However, MacArthur complained to Washington of 'unparalleled conditions of restraint and handicap' on his Korean command.[†]

Ever willing to do MacArthur's bidding, the new US Eighth Army commander, General Ridgway, launched Operation Ripper on 7 March. A week later Seoul was retaken and the 38th Parallel reached, where the UN forces had been in October 1950. MacArthur now desperately wanted to strike north again, so his response to the message, below, from the JCS on 20 March, bought a simple request for fewer military restrictions on his command:

State Department planning a Presidential announcement shortly that, with clearing bulk of South Korea of aggressors, United Nations now preparing to

---

[*]   Robert Frank Futrell, *The United States Air Force in Korea, 1950–1953* (Progressive Management, 1983).

[†]   James McGovern, *To the Yalu: From the Chinese Invasion of Korea to MacArthur's Dismissal* (William Morrow, New York, 1972).

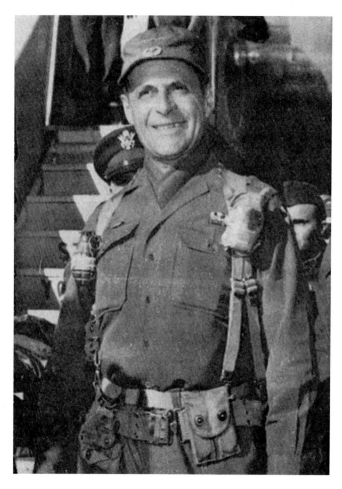

Matthew Ridgway in 1951.

discuss conditions of settlement in Korea. United Nations feeling exists that further diplomatic efforts towards settlement should be made before any advance with major forces north of 38th Parallel. Time will be required to determine diplomatic reactions and permit new negotiations that may develop. Recognizing that parallel had no military significance, State has asked Joint Chiefs what authority you should have to permit sufficient freedom of action for next few weeks to provide security for United Nations forces and maintain contact with enemy. Your recommendations desired.*

The proposed announcement by President Truman would, in part, say that a 'prompt settlement of the Korean problem would greatly reduce international tension in the Far

---

* Ibid.

East and would open the way for consideration of other problems in that area by the processes of peaceful settlement envisaged in the Charter of the United Nations'.*

Ignoring Washington's directive of 6 December 1950 for all actions to be approved by the administration, on 24 March General MacArthur issued a unilateral statement that was tantamount to giving Beijing an ultimatum:

> The enemy, therefore, must by now be fully aware that a decision of the United Nations to depart from its tolerant effort to contain the war to the area of Korea, through an expansion of our military operations to its coastal areas and interior bases, would doom Red China to the risk of imminent military failure. [I am] ready at any time to confer in the field with the Commander-in-chief of the enemy forces in earnest effort to find any military means whereby realization of the political objectives of the United Nations in Korea, to which no nation may justly take exceptions, might be accomplished without further bloodshed.†

In the White House, President Truman heard of his general's statement with incredulity and anger. Whilst MacArthur believed his was merely a military assessment, his commander-in-chief had had enough of his open defiance and insubordination. Embarrassment for the Truman administration ensued, as many of his friends in the West questioned what they perceived to be a sudden shift in foreign policy regarding the Korean issue.

Beijing's reaction was unequivocal, the government-owned radio stating:

> Warmonger MacArthur made a fanatical but shameless statement with the intention of engineering the Anglo-American aggressors to extend the war of aggression into China. MacArthur's shameless tricks ... will meet with failure. The people of China must raise their sense of vigilance by doubling their effort for the sacred struggle.

China would not contemplate sitting at the negotiation table for another two years. From late March to early April 1951, the CPVA offered the advancing UN forces increased resistance, especially along the central front in the Kap'yŏng and Ch'unch'ŏn areas. Within supporting distance of the front, the Chinese built up a powerful reserve force, which included four fresh North Korean corps, totalling twelve divisions, six fresh CPVA corps totalling eighteen divisions, and four CPVA corps recently withdrawn from combat.

The most intense fighting would take place along the Hant'anch'ŏn River east of its confluence with the Imjin, along the southern approached to the Hwach'ŏn Reservoir,

---

* Ibid.
† Ibid.

American prisoners of war captured by the Chinese.

and along the Soyang River a few miles to the east. Throughout this period, in a build-up to the launching of their fifth offensive, there was a continuous movement of combat forces into forward areas, with daily vehicle sightings frequently passing the 2,000 mark.

In his sixth and final volume in a series on battles of the Korean War, the author will look at continued conflict on the 38th Parallel, including a disaster for British forces. A war of attrition would become the order of the day, with a marked increase in the air war.

There would also be a parting of the ways between Truman and MacArthur.

BIBLIOGRAPHY

1st Marine Division Historical Diary – November 1950 (National Archives and Records Administration, College Park Maryland).

1st Marine Division Special Action Diary – October 1950–December 1950 (National Archives and Records Administration, College Park Maryland).

27th British Commonwealth Brigade War Diary September to November 1950 (The Australia War Memorial archives, Campbell).

3rd Battalion, The Royal Australian War Diary November 1950. (The Australia War Memorial archives, Campbell)

Boose, Donald W. Jnr, *US Army Forces in the Korean War* (Osprey Publishing, Oxford, 2005).

Central Intelligence Agency (CIA) declassified documents.

Cunningham-Boothe, Ashley and Peter Farrar, Eds., *British Forces in the Korean War* (British Korean Veterans Association, 1997).

Fehrenbach, T.R., *This Kind of War: The Classic Korean War History* (Potomac Books, 2000).

Futrell, Robert Frank, *The United States Air Force in Korea, 1950–1953* (Progressive Management, 1983).

Gugeler, Russell A., *Combat Actions in Korea* (Center of Military History, United States Army, Washington D.C., 1954).

Hastings, Max, *The Korean War* (Pan, London, 1987).

Korean War Project, www.koreanwar.org/

Knox, Donald, *The Korean War, Pusan to Chosin: An Oral History* (Harcourt Brace & Co., Orlando, 1985).

Latham, William Clark, *Cold Days in Hell: American POWs in Korea* (Texas A&M University Press, 2013).

Mao, Min, *Marshal Peng De-huai* (2018).

McGovern, James, *To the Yalu, From the Chinese Invasion of Korea to MacArthur's Dismissal* (William Morrow, New York, 1972).

Montross, L., et al, *U.S. Marine Operations in Korea, 1950–1953* (US Government Printing Office, Washington, 1962).

US Navy, US Marine Corps and Coast Guard historical offices, *The Sea Services in the Korean War, 1950–1953* (US Naval Institute, Annapolis, 1957, 2000).

Tucker, Spencer C., Ed., *Encyclopedia of the Korean War* (Checkmark Books, New York, 2002).

United Nations Command, Military Intelligence Section, *Korea, A Summary 25 June 1950–25 April 1952.*

United States Army Records, National Archives and Records Administration (NARA), College Park, Maryland, USA.

van Tonder, Gerry, *North Korea Invades the South: Across the 38th Parallel, June 1950* (Pen and Sword Military, Barnsley, 2018).

van Tonder, Gerry, *North Korean Onslaught: UN Stand at the Pusan Perimeter, August–September 1950.* (Pen and Sword Military, Barnsley, 2018).

van Tonder, Gerry, *Inchon Landing: MacArthur's Korean War Masterstroke, September 1950* (Pen and Sword Military, Barnsley, 2019).

van Tonder, Gerry, *Korean War: Allied Surge: Pyongyang Falls, UN Sweep to the Yalu, October 1950.* (Pen and Sword Military, Barnsley, 2019).

War Diary X Corps Monthly Summary 1 Oct 1950 to 31 Oct 1950.

Weintraub, Stanley, *A Christmas Far from Home: An Epic Tale of Courage and Survival during the Korean War* (Hachette, UK, 2014)

Whiting, Allen S., *China Crosses the Yalu: The Decision to Enter the Korean War.* (Stanford University Press, Stanford, 1968).

Index

About the Author

Born in Southern Rhodesia, now Zimbabwe, historian and author Gerry van Tonder came to Britain in 1999. Specializing in military history, Gerry started his writing career with titles about twentieth-century guerrilla and open warfare in southern Africa, including the co-authored definitive *Rhodesia Regiment 1899–1981*. Gerry presented a copy of this title to the regiment's former colonel-in-chief, Her Majesty the Queen. Having written over twenty books, Gerry writes extensively for several Pen & Sword military history series including 'Cold War 1945–1991', 'Military Legacy' (focusing on the heritage of British cities), 'Echoes of the Blitz', and 'History of Terror'.

Other titles by Gerry van Tonder

Berlin Blockade: Soviet Chokehold and the Great Allied Airlift 1948–1949
Chesterfield's Military Heritage
Derby in 50 Buildings
Echoes of the Coventry Blitz
Inchon Landing: MacArthur's North Korean Masterstroke, September 1950
Irgun: Revisionist Zionism 1931–1948
Korean War: Allied Surge: Pyongyang Falls, UN Sweep to the Yalu, October 1950
Lt-Gen Keith Coster: A Life in Uniform
Malayan Emergency: Triumph of the Running Dogs 1948–1960
Mansfield Through Time
North Korea Invades the South: Across the 38th Parallel, June 1950
North Korean Onslaught: UN Stand at the Pusan Perimeter August-September 1950
*North of the Red Line: Recollections of the Border War by Members of the South African
    Armed Forces: 1966–1989*
Nottingham's Military Legacy
Operation Lighthouse: Intaf in the Rhodesian Bush War 1972–1980
Red China: Mao Crushes Chiang's Kuomintang, 1949
Rhodesia Regiment 1899–1981
Rhodesian African Rifles/Rhodesia Native Regiment Book of Remembrance
Rhodesian Combined Forces Roll of Honour 1966-1981
Sheffield's Military Legacy
Sino-Indian War: October–November 1962
SS Einsatzgruppen: Nazi Death Squads 1939–1945